For my father, James Dillon,

who loved without measure

Table of Contents

Destiny
Devil Trails
The Dictator
The Director
The Disenchanted
Disguises
Distress
A Divine Romance
Divine Union
Divinity Think
Doubting Thomas Crisscrossed India
A Down Home Christmas
The Doyenne of Society
Dreaming
The Dream of Love
The Dynamic of the West

Earthbound
Eden Revisited
Embers
To Emily
Encounter by Jade Mountain
An Engineer Entrepreneur
The Eternal One
The Extra-Terrestrial

Fabled Waters
The Fairy Fête
Faithful to the Cross
Fall Sowing
The Father
A Faust Reverie
Fireflies
The Fisher King
Flower Talk
The Forests of Carmel

John Paul II
Joseph
Julian
The Junior Partner

Kimono Moon
Kimono Snow
Kinesis

Lady of Clairvaux
The Lady of the Lake
Lake Chartreuse
Lament
Laurels
Lawrence of Arabia
The Legacy
The Letter Child
Levitating
Lightning
Little valentines dropped out the sky
Living Above the Natural Level
A Loft
The Lord of History
The Lost Thought
The Lost Wedding
The Love Insurrection
Love in the Desert
The Love Project
The Lover
Love spoke out in ancient Palestine
Love's Strategy
Love was born in Bethlehem
Low Tide
Loyola
Lucubrations

Lullaby Lake
Lullaby Sky
Lullaby Wind

The Madonna Painting
Mapling in the North Country
To Mary
Mater Orphanorum
Mellifont
Memories of a Country Childhood
Merry Ireland
The Microdot Worm
Midnight Tryst
Migrations
My Mind a Rookery
Mingling
A Miscalculation
Mist
Moments
The Moonflower
Morning Trail
In a Mountain Valley
The Music Lover

The National Birthday
The Nightingale Floor
Nights
The Night Watch
Nocturne
The Noncollaboration
November Tryst
Now as a ghost of quaint-remembered time

The Retreatmaster
The Reunion
Reverie on Music
Romance in the Black Forest
The Round Tower
Ryedale

The Sadist
My Sainted Mother
Saint Lucy's Day
Saint Martin's Summer
Saint Merry
Saint Valentine
Saint Virgil
Salzburg
Scholar Days
The Scholar Knight
The Schoolmistress
The Seaport
The Secret of Happiness
Serendipity
The Shamrock Lady
The Shepherd Boy
The Shepherd Lad
The Siege of Belgrade, 1456
Since first you broached you would a voyage make
The Sky Dweller
Sky Pillows
Snares
The Snow Maiden
The Song of Demeter
A Southern Belle
Spaces
The Starfisher
The Stoic
Strayed sapients

Wanderers Nachtlied
When Aelred walked the valley of the Rye
When a voyager in this heady place of dreams
When evening trips across the starry sky
When first we met in labyrinthine night
When I all alone in somber sorrow sit
When in the course of unrelenting time
When in the fray of a wayward and chaotic time
When in the grip of a wild and darkling night
When in the reminisce of a long-forgotten time
When in the retrospect of a distant time
When in the vise of elder-drifting time
When in the winter of our experiment
When summer faints upon an autumn trail
When the fruits to labor are denied
When thoughts immortal descend to mortal strand
Wild Swans
A Winter Child
A Winter Field
The Winter Plum Tree
The Winter Sea
A Winter Sprite
A Wintry Fantasy
A Win-Win Game
A Wonder
The Woolies
A Worldly Maneuver
The Worldly Young Governor of Perugia
World Youth Day in Madrid, 2011

Young Artist Relations

The Abbey

A schoolmistress lessons us in Lamartine
      On mild September days
While lazy squirrels careless drop their acorns
      On russet-fashioned sprays.

O temps, suspends ton vol! et vous, heures propices,
      Suspendez votre cours!
Laissez-nous savourer les rapides délices
      Des plus beaux de nos jours!

I converse with you in Alexandrine rhyme,
      Rambling on the lawn,
And evenings travel amid French novelties
      Until the touch of dawn.

While I learn the folkways of a sophomore,
      A heavenly child peeps out a golden door.

The Academy

We friended young in garlanded, fir-trimmed halls,
Where master practiced us in olden song.
We mused on rounds of festive Christmas balls
And jested free in jolly hockey throng.

I remember how we played at patient scholars,
Traipsed at leisure through old French châteaux,
Worked out probability in dollars,
And read the sayings of a Cicero.

We chatted o'er the howls of the Grendel troll
And climbed the networks of a mathematician,
While snow fell soft on that Advent knoll,
And in loving wise mothered the tradition.

Acting Class

On Sundays we gather
To do mad Hamlet's eternal question
Or the ages of man
Or even the matchmaker's reasons
For arranging her own match
Lady Macbeth's perversity
And the importance of really being in earnest throughout.

And over it all presides Sir William
Whose reminisce leaps
From a leading lady chauffeuring a sick chauffeur
To being kissed in a ragman's outfit before the maître de.

Advent at the College of St. Elizabeth

A gaggle of geese pecks fodder on the lawn,
Their webprints in patches of lambent snow.
I peer from storied library
To gaze upon the gray-cold vale below.

A lone thespian paces the proscenium
Of a Greek theater to winter's faint applaud.
I overhear a rustle of foreign tongues
That exchanges secrets in accents grown abroad.

Christmas reigns in the festooned lobby below.
A fir tree bears an angel diadem.
Outside the geese snuggle in the snow.
I reflect in prayer on a winter in Bethlehem.

"All night thunder"

All night thunder
Booms off the ramparts of heaven.

I in my garret
Snuggle warm.

"All's winter now about my heart"

All's winter now about my heart
Since first of love you lost the darling art.
A wind blows surly on the barren plain.
An eagle huddles in the sunlight wane
And silent broods upon a darkening bough,
Full naked to the world has fallen now.
You were subdued by the enticements of a foe
Who offered charms to turn your heart to snow.
I stoke the hearth with pine and crackling oak
And recall your love for neighboring gentlefolk.
I remember late the divine and kindly sue
That courts a waif from frostbite turning blue.
As sure as faith and love have bound us twain,
You shall warm your heart by mine again.

Ambrosia

Enmeshed in chocolates and strawberry sundaes,
She drowned her cares in decaffeinated tea.
Warm and safe in her fashionable christening gown,
From friends she enjoyed warmest courtesy.

In musty tomes she chanced upon her saint
Who fasted to pay the arrears of his members lay.
She read how Ambrose maneuvered his congregation
Past the quicksands of imperial power play.

Now the empress mother was an Arian
And craved to ensconce her inimical heresy,
But commoners barricaded the basilica doors
Against the siege of imperial soldiery.

Ambrose divided the defenders into alternate choirs
And taught them to sing the hymns he had composed.
All Holy Week they sang beneath the spires
While the surrounding army hapless vigilled and dozed.

On Easter Day the emperor withdrew,
Impressed by the faithful's constant ecstasy.
Ordinary folk had withstood the imperial pride,
Had fasted and prayed in mystic rhapsody.

Ambrosia pondered the witness of history
And fathomed the thrust of Ambrose' passionate prayer.
She fasted from the delights of the palate
And set her feet upon the mystic stair.

"An angel tapped on my icicle door"

An angel tapped on my icicle door
And sang some chapel lays.
I opened wide to all her lore
And found my hearth ablaze.

She beamed a loving prayer to me
And displayed kind children's ways.
She joked among the villagery
To banish vinegar days.

The Angelus

Sounds the hour
Bell in a tower.

A weeping family tree
Stuck together elbow to knee.

Sounds the hour
Angel with a flower.

Heaven in the sound
Hope on the ground.

Sounds the hour
Falls a graceful shower.

Prayer cushions create space
Breathing room in a family place.

Sounds the hour
Heaven in a maiden's bower.

"Angel voice"

Angel voice
   Midnight rejoice
      Love pokes through to the world.

The Arboretum

A cherry tree gnarls.
   Windflowers blow in a Shakespeare garden.
      We dance in conversation rings.

"As autumn hastened by with fragile look"

As autumn hastened by with fragile look
While we were smiling on a distant spire,
She glanced not robust but a wizened guest
That faded at the crackle of a fire.

I failed to catch her in her airy sweep.
She danced upon the chance and antic wind,
Flaunted tatters of a glory hue
And with my spirits melancholy twinned.

The Ascetics

In the depths of night Love burst out.

Angels as immaterial as Love
Heard of the divine child.

Transported by thoughts,
They announced a Messiah in a manger
To shepherds living a hardscrabble life.

Deserts away, a star commenced its trek.
Their angels whispering the birth of a king,
Wealthy astrologers scrambled their camels
And journeyed by night into mystery.

"As daylight shifts across the evening sky"

As daylight shifts across the evening sky,
And lakes shimmer in the sunset flair,
A monastery bell then calls to prayer.
When the sweet birds sing a lullaby,
My soul floats up an invisible heavenly stair
And thinks beyond the trajectory of the moon.
The nuns will fall upon their pillows soon,
But now I tiptoe spy to watch their prayer.
The tower bell chimes quiet time at last,
And flowers shut a weary daydream eye.
I discern that Love envelops us by and by
And note their gaze turned forward by a fast.
When all the world has gone to bed away,
Then saints in vigil for divine compassion pray.

"As evening creeps upon the darkening stair"

As evening creeps upon the darkening stair,
And shadows make their fateful, black descend,
I turn to You, O God, my soul's repair,
And think our gulf of thought and will to end.
You are my all, my own, my native land,
My true country, redemption's final end,
You Who wrote a magic in a grain of sand,
A love letter in a flower to send.
Why yield I not at heaven's brightest port?
Why hold I yet aloof from giving all?
Why can I not think celestial sport
Or answer when I hear the angel's call?
I love You truly and would myself erase.
Sweet Saviour, help me win the eternal race.

"As now across the distant sky you've sped"

As now across the distant sky you've sped,
No more to trod your own, your native land,
So I on the margent grim and chastened tread
And figure moments lost upon the sand.
I thought our love to be the enduring kind;
You broke with me as if you had no heart.
My soul spoke loud and you did shut your mind;
Your windows all did close against my dart.
I stay here narrow while you chart abroad
And wonder at the gain that you have found,
The bewitching fame that made your promise flawed.
I am sad surprised you are no longer bound.
I shoot a prayer into the starry void
And aim it at suspense that we have toyed.

The Astrologers

The observatory stood on a lonely oasis hill
Where stars cast down their silent spears of light.
Three astrologers sought their dreams to fulfill,
Made observations on the grand sidereal sight.

So passed the evening. The stars shone cold and bright.
Orion hunted bears across the sky.
The astrologers tracked his moving shards of light.
Cassiopeia vaunted her beauty on high.

They fell betimes a-slumber and had a dream
Of a light shimmering from the firmament.
A voice bade them pursue the wondrous beam
To discover a king in childhood's raiment.

When they awoke, a shaft of light ran
Adrift a rift beneath the starry pale.
Slowly it traveled west. A caravan
They gathered to shadow its luminescent trail.

They passed through desert and tilted pasturelands,
Confiding in grace through vast, uncharted sands.
They had ventured out in risky history.
They trusted when all about was mystery.

An Athenian in Sparta

I am trapped in an avalanche of snow
Till love does melt this existential low.

I crave the distant beauty of the spring,
Apple blooms and Oriental cherry.
They blow graceful in another vale.
I have no way here to make merry.

Eternal Wisdom guards scholars in their towers
Where their souls can grow in lasting amity,
Shall I stay forever in the paralyzing snow
Or lose myself in bonds of charity?

My judge acquits me yet imperfectly
Like a humble, plodding, miscreant bumblebee
Cancelled in the mews of history,
Brushed by the ash of mistaken revelry.

My brothers random speak in Plato's tongue
Of star sailors en route to their mother city.
My sister steads me o'er a trembling stream.
The kindness of friends checks my melancholy.

I was trapped in an avalanche of snow
Till love did melt my existential low.

Autumn in Beijing

A melancholy moon afloat the sky
      Lit our rowboat quiet by.
North Lake was filled with happy craft.
      On a neighbor skiff kindly friendship laughed.

Where are you, O autumn night,
      That rippled poetry did lend.
You've flown away on zephyr's wings,
      Bestowed a blessing in farewell end.

You lettered me from afar
      In accents warm dispensed with love.
You chatted through the traps of cynics.
      Nested in friendship's tryst a dove.

To refresh my soul I long to see
The friend who's now mere memory.

Autumn Leaves

The vermilion castaways of maple stands
      Grace the river like floating gondolas
That hazard a voyage to exotic lands
      Past our anchored pergolas.

Autumn Song

As summer exits now in sunny state
And crimson leaves o'er the meadow drift,
I gaze again upon the signs of autumn
As russet riots whirl in wayward rift.
The trees that in the spring white petals bore,
And all the trails of summer draped in green,
Now against a bright October sky
Display their flairs as on a sunset screen.
Thou, too, in fairest russet dressed
Ne'er looked so radiant and jocose.
This raiment turns all eyes upon thee now,
A diamond found among the throng morose.
Yet harvest love while the sap runs mellow
In medley with thy heart's most faithful fellow.

The Bachelor Scholar

I wrap in meditate the dapple-faced dawn
And watch the frost turn leaves to apricot hue.

The canal is cluttered by the falling throng;
I feel a pang for its glory days.

Shells are racing through the daybreak mist;
The river startles in the October wind.

I am fragile in this pageant
As I will not attend another autumn.

The Banquet

Candlelight, crystal and flowers preside
O'er words that march on trochee light.
Diamonds and medals classify
While livery stands at the idle polite.

Friendship warms in anecdotal flow
And rapier wit in verbal toss and throw.
But I see all this as through a mystic veil
While I commune with Love in light beyond the pale.

Barbara

She met both her husbands on the same night.
John romanced her and danced her
And one day asked Frank to be best man at the wedding.

Then John passed on
And Frank came by to comfort the widow.
"He was the best man after all," she said.

Frank died on the eve of the Depression
So Barbara went to work in the dress section
Of a fashionable department store.

She raised two small children at night.
Her son went off to World War II.
Her daughter married a would-be entrepreneur.

At length she reached the grandmother stage,
Crocheting baby clothes, mittens, doilies and afghans
For her children, friends and the church bazaar.

She took me to see Hamlet,
A blond lad who struck a classic pose
And said so many things that sounded familiar.

Envoi

When her life began to close
And come to a timely end,
She abandoned all her natural ways
And sainted made ascend.

The Battle of Muret, 1213

The gnostic Albigensians were battling for Languedoc
In their rebellion against Christian France.
Simon de Montfort was fighting for the realm
When Peter of Aragon saw his chance.

At the town of Muret Peter with forty thousand
Besieged de Montfort's trusty eight hundred,
And the battle seemed over before it began.
De Montfort's men counted themselves as dead.

Saint Dominic and other gentility
Hastened to the church and lay on the pavement prostrate,
Begging for mercy and improbable victory.
In God's Hands they placed the Christians' fate.

De Montfort sent his cavalry on the attack,
Counseling against single combat in the fight.
Arrogant Aragon, fresh from a night of wenching,
Exchanged his armor with a lowly knight.

When the French felled his vassal, he mocked their error.
With "the king is *here*" he declared his royalty.
The French knights then hacked their way to him,
And he forthwith became a date in history.

Disheartened by the knights of Christian France,
The enemy broke ranks and fled in direst dread.
Nearly half the foe drowned or were impaled.
Peace was the legacy of the regretful dead.

In the battle only one French knight had died.
Dominic and his friends God's favor did provide.

Beaupré

Falls the November rain
On Stoic philosophy.
'Twixt the cliff and a mirror sea
Lies tattered memory.

To a childhood rendezvous
I return after half a century.
The rest were waylaid
Somewhere in history.

But you still reside in your castle
'Twixt the cliff and a mirror sea.
You o'erlook fault lines
In mildest charity.

Beauty

A peony opened ruby white
Its feather petals to catch the morning dew,
And I, breathless at the lovely sight,
Forgot my wilding tale of somber rue.

For I in jungle glare had lived,
Scratched by thistle and by thorn.
Fretful woe had I full measure sieved
And joy forgot, all fragile and forlorn.

I think these flower feathers yield fair promise
To those who look for sights unknown
For Beauty yet lives when all's amiss
In seeds of life eternal sown.

The Beloved

She came morose and tattered to the shrine
Where for an hour on Wednesdays she faithfully prayed.
She entered the chapel and abashed fell to her knees
And before the Lord her concerns and fears displayed.

The nuns were engaged elsewhere in discussions,
And she was alone in the Divine Presence.
She plunged into intense mystical prayer,
Asking a blessing on her constituents.

Angels choired in joyous eternity
While she implored favors from the Divinity.
Friends reported miracles from time to time.

"O dear God, I adore and love you so.
Help my children in Your grace to grow."

She emerged resplendent in a starry gown.

The Bethlehem Child

In a midnight stable was the birth
Of Nature's King upon the earth.
He lay in a manger on random hay.
Thus Love was born on Christmas Day.

Our God became poor and frail
So of His creatures none should fail
To find that love's worth more than gold
And heaven lasts beyond the old.

Sweet Mary laughed to see her Boy.
Her weary heart was changed to joy.
She cradled the sun before the morn
When Love into history was born.

Bethlehem Moments

Millennia ago in backwater Bethlehem
A virgin mother kept the wolves at bay
With prayer and fasts and kindly words and deeds.

Caught in the web of time, we hide in nooks and crannies
Until with miracles she visits the earth
To encourage our prayer and fasts and kindly words and deeds.

The Birch Trees

Some birch trees on a sky-blue October day
In helianthin flame their exiting addressed.
Beyond a fortress crouched in stone-cold gray.

The orange leaves of these trees, their time expressed,
Wafted on flights of air to the earth
And our thoughts with eternity impressed.

Partial to this brilliant sunset mirth,
We reminisce the invisible Deity
Whose painterly skills bring Beauty to the earth.

Linger on, blest phenomenon,
As men grope their way through the ashen.

The Blind Poet

With Homer's failing was I blessed.
When rosy fingers play at dawn
On lyre striated in the sky,
I alone am unimpressed,
Attending dawn with a yawn,
The inflamed heavens with a sigh,
For I in eternal night am plunged
And never see the break of day.
From my sight are expunged
Vermilion clouds at their play.
Then Love invisible comes gently mingling,
In this crook of the universe lambent tingling.
Where creviced night with pain doth rend,
Haply God with dreams doth make amend.

The Bolero

When midnight chimes awake a dancing choir,
And shapes of ghosts across the brain do mull,
Faithless daydreams stay to wayward lull,
And love departs from out a troubled spire.

Though tutored choir forgets its Latin score,
I everywhere dance on constant cloudlet mellow
Lest I lose a merry love-sped fellow
And float away to drowsy lotus shore.

I think the chary heart does the self contain
And spirals not for unmelodic rote,
But patient awaits the wild paseo note,
Then walks assured and stamps the glad refrain.

Love spent, tumbledown, I mirror this dream
And chance in your eyes a light agleam.

Carmela*

She was a pretty, loving personality
Out of an Italian home in village America.
Mornings she rode the Staten Island ferry
To the sophisticated venues of Wall Street exotica.

There she bonded to the upper class,
But found she was in the servant game
And lacked the credentials to ascend the social ladder,
The initials a man might wear after his name.

She fought off the zombies and their takeover bids
And drew the circle close of family and friends.
She rose into the spiritual upper class,
Understood the times and dubious trends.

She legacied for young folks a scholarship lift,
Put in their biographies more upward drift.

*Carmela D'Alessio

38

Cashel Castle

On Saint Patrick's Day a fair company had gathered
To chat away the evening by the fire.
Mirth and cheer in that exuberant society
Chased away anxious thoughts and tears.
Witty points flashed in the vibrant air
While hilarity winked in every eye,
A laugh upon the heart caught unaware.

Then Michael rose to tell an olden tale
Of when Patrick approached the Irish shore
To bring the learning of the Latin race
And rescue men from sullen heathen trace
So that love would beat in every Christian breast.
He came to make them children of the light
And point them to an everlasting rest.

In the days when Patrick took the ancient fire
From southern clime and brought it over to Eire,
King Aengus of Munster reigned from Cashel Castle,
Contented master of his pagan realm.
He loved to hunt the valleys after game,
In search of deer and rabbit to support the throng
Of friends and relatives within his hall.

When the tidings came that Patrick was in Tara,
King Aengus pondered long upon the matter.
He thought to change his cult but had no will.
His nobles and his kin were all opposed.
Then Patrick to his Cashel stronghold came.
King Aengus trembled in his cup of mead,
A benighted man held by an ancestral claim.

That night the idols crashed within the walls.
In fragments broke the olden druid gods.
The king awoke to see the sorry sight.
The court was in a flutter all amazed.
Then Aengus swore to suppress the pagan rite,
To accept the Faith that miracles had wrought
And retrieve the land from wild and demon night.

At dawn went Aengus with his noble clan
To greet the saint and stand his host in all.
Patrick bade him bow to Divinity
And held as pattern for the Trinity
A shamrock in his consecrated hand.
He poured blessed water on king and retinue
And offered Mass for all in Munster land.

The king was charmed to wash in christening rain.
The shadow realm rushed out his windy soul.
He felt the fine and holy mirth that gentles
Souls who prosper on the way to heaven.
Before the vast assemblage Aengus swore
To govern wisely and champion the poor
Until he came to yon eternal shore.

So Michael ended his tale to lusty cheers.
The company complimented him with zest
And reminisced the store of Irish lore.
Around the hearth spoke mirth in every eye.
There love was matched with swift reciprocity.
Charity induced the conversation
And kindness reigned o'er the company.

The Castle

Once there was a castle
Built in a country town,
And deep within the fortress
Lived squires and their gown.

They bustled around the ramparts,
Secured them fast and strong.
They sallied forth in society
And did no neighbor wrong.

One day there came a damsel
Who wore a different dress.
They welcomed her in friendship
And felt no more distress.

A foreign pair was hired
To watch the castle grounds.
They smiled and laughed a lot
And made caretaking rounds.

I thought there was a lesson
Within this tale of old.
It's when you play life gentle
That gentle ends unfold.

Castle Chartreuse

In my solitary I pray you, love, do tarry
For I seek you out the buffoon, fadding throng.
I fly your banner o'er the rampart strong
And think upon the day when we did marry.

'Twas a May morn with nary a cloud in the sky,
And blossoms tossed upon a fitful breeze.
The daisies chachaed in a merry tease,
And tulips tangoed with the lilies shy.

What will you do for love, you piquant asked.
I'll give up all I hold most dear.
That rupture might have cost me many a tear,
But that love wielded the sword so valiant tasked.

I'll ne'er forget sweet heaven's thrust and parry
To win for me a love so friendly vary.

The Cave

An angel led me far abroad
On tiptoe past a drowsy town
Lustred by a lantern moon.

At last I found a stable flawed
And there left behind a skeptic frown
On the threshold with my nothing shoon.

Chartreuse

In mountain fast full of secret herb
Range the edelweiss slender and superb.
They mingle dew against the tiger wilds
While slumber light the carefree daisy milds.
By day the daisies wake and playful pelt
The edelweiss that love enhancing spelt
For none does know that in love there lurks a song
That steads the leas high above the throng,
And that the edelweiss once swept away,
Crimson-decked the meadows weep that day.
Raging through a rude and savage beast
Would pluck each flower for a fiery feast
While now at parties on the meandering Thames
Pours amaranth down some lacy stems.

The Chatelaine

She writes upon the sky the name of friend
To me whom the world finds a trifle shy.
When I languish from disappointment without end,
I rest a while or two within her eye.

She rescues me from dangling in the grays
And sets me high within her sovereign play.
Her compassionate heart relies on the Ancient of Days.
I have no way to repay this my cradle stay.

Cherry Lake

I flashed the light in their eyes,
  And the frogs were mesmerized.

A Filipina from the bayou country waded into the muck
  And wrung each little froggy neck.

That night I slept tight in my bed.
  The chorus of frogs was dead.

The Cherubs

The church is bedecked with candles and flowers.
A rosy flame flickers in the sanctuary,
And all the angels are attentive.

Families take their seats with high expectation.
Little angels sit here and there
Next to their charges, the better to whisper.

There is singing, and the cherubs sing along.
The children kneel, and their angels kneel also.
The children pray, and the cherubs attend each murmur.

Then the bells ring.
The cherubs prostrate, their wings a-flutter,
Because God is coming, and they are so happy.

After Mass the children talk to their friends,
And the cherubs bobble around in happiness.

The Child King

His life began so poor,
        But heralded by a star,
Swaddling clothes to keep him warm,
        But angels in attend.

His visitors were shepherds low
        And wise men from afar.
He lay all night without the inn,
        The king of love unend.

Children

Sabina was expecting her first child
And thought she should find out what to do.
She consulted Julianne who had a lot of offspring
On how to raise her child without any rue.

"Children start out loving their families,"
Said her friend most merrily,
"But then someone trains them
On how to treat their family.

"Parents who take the Ten Commandments
As the guidelines of their lives
Communicate love to their children
And don't get into serial wives."

Sabina took this advice seriously,
And the rest of her life turned out happily.

Choices

The father was a smoker who sold cars.
The son chose a different path.

As a boy, he met St. André Bessette who worked miracles.
Impressed, he left his nickel wealth behind a church pillar.

He obtained a bachelor's degree in chemical engineering,
But they advised him that research was not his vocation.

He took a Jesuit priest as his role model
Which gave him motivation and upward lift.

He watched a television series on the War in the Pacific
Because his brother had gone through hellfire there.

He admired Horatio for singlehandedly repelling the Etruscans
While old men cut down the bridge behind him.

He recalled Robert the Bruce who watched a spider
Repeatedly toss its thread across a void before it took hold.

He listened to Strauss waltzes and the highlights of "Carmen"
And hung Rosa Bonheur's "The Horse Fair" in his living room.

He conversed daily with the Beyond,
Tithed, and was kind to all he met.

Eventually he headed up research and development
At a chemical company as well as mergers and acquisitions.

The Christmas Angels

Lofty lights murmured expectantly.
A laugh coalesced around a nimbus flight.
The happy ones dropped down to earth below
And pastored shepherds through the Bethlehem night.

The Christmas Child

A baby lies
        'Neath wuthering skies.
                The Messiah we adore.

An infant bright
        Hovered round with light
                From the prophets' lore.

Heaven's disguise
        For artless eyes
                Hides a transcendent shore.

A Christmas Fête in the Library

Where oft I reveled in a book
And all my daily cares forsook
While old tomes musted in fragrant mounds,
Now a Mistletoe Fairy stilt-dancing clowns.

Luscious Gruyère and ambrosia combine.
The company mellows as they sip their wine
And listen to the story of a Christmas in Wales
By a firelit hearth that flickers, then fails.

A waltz band sweetly seduces the sedate
Under murals of printers balancing plate,
Moses readying God's Writ to throw,
And monks copying on against Norse flambeaux.

And all my fabulous friends in books
Are guarding their secrets against passer-by looks.

The Church of Saint Bathilda

Wisps of snow were falling in the great metropolis
Where townhouses and pieds-à-terre
Clustered intimately against one another.
Snowflakes floated nonchalantly to earth
Noticed only by the children.

In a church on the rue Beaumont
A tiny flame fluttered in the sanctuary.
In the shadows Saint Anthony conversed with the Child Jesus,
Saint Anne was teaching Mary how to read,
And Queen Bathilda smiled benevolently.

Stained-glass colors shifted imperceptibly
Over the flagstones in the nave.
Sequestered souls wandered in their thoughts.
Only God was privy to their distractions.
He listened and sometimes He spoke.

Outside the snow floated tranquilly
As twilight approached the outskirts of the city.
Within the people were finishing their prayers.
The saints continued their occupations,
And the devil was noticeably absent.

The Church of Saint Ives

Twilight was about to envelop the village
When I went for a stroll in the streets.
I had seen at a certain distance from the village
An old church and I was curious about it.

A sign informed me that Saint Ives presided there.
The well-tended cemetery dated from the last century.
At random I pushed the door
And found it was unlocked. I entered.

A flame was dancing in the sanctuary,
And the vigil lights near the Virgin Mary
Were reminding her of her childrens' requests.
A bouquet of flowers was spreading its fragrance.

I sat down in the shadows
And set myself to pray.

When I awoke,
The bell was sounding midnight.
A ghost was advancing slowly
Down the center aisle toward the sanctuary.

When it arrived at the communion rail,
It began to whisper its prayers.
My heart pounding wildly,
I approached the mystery.

The phantom did not notice me.
It was too busy rehearsing its sins -
The prayers it had omitted
During its adventures on earth.

It had yet years of vigils to do
To pay for its carelessness so dear.

The Church of Saint Wulphy

Saint Wulphy looked benevolently around the church.
Here and there a Wulphy sat in the pews.
The Holy Cross Boys Choir of Neuilly
Was singing a hymn from long ago.

> Wounded by holy love and in horror
> Of the dangerous love of the world,
> He followed to the end
> The steep road that leads to heaven.

These words recalled to Wulphy his life in the seventh century
When he would stroll about the village a man like other men.
He was married and had some children fairly grown
When his neighbors elected him pastor.

> Mastering his flesh by fasts
> And nourishing his soul
> On the sweet sustenance of prayer,
> He won the joys of heaven.

Wulphy saw the hand of God in this mandate.
With the consent of his wife,
He decided to follow this new vocation,
But he found the ascetic life difficult.

> May all be pure in our hearts,
> May malice be banished,
> May moderation in drinking and eating
> Subdue the pride of the flesh.

Wulphy decided to leave for the Holy Land
In order to change his lifestyle.
Upon his return he lived an ascetic in the woods
And became a miracle worker.

Now the saint noted the joyous sounds
And how happy the Wulphys were in their pews.

The City of Light

The poesy of Jeanne Marie
Falls for the mysteries around Old Paris.

She imagines students in medieval gown
Clustering in cloisters to chat about the town.

She who dresses in rational modern fashion
Is cognizant of the grace of the Sainte Chapelle.

Mademoiselle with a laugh inside
Puzzles o'er the enigmatic Mona Lisa.

She climbs the storied streets of Montmartre,
Fascined by the imagine of its artists at their paints.

She delights in the buttresses of Notre Dame,
A mass of stone anchored by the Seine.

But, Jeanne, the imps on rainy days
Envy your immortal ways.

Climbing

I crash through the brambles between us
Loving is my life

We clamber through the muddy deep
Such price the stars

We climb beyond the village circuitry
And from our mountain aerie
Pluck bold visions from the glorious skies

A Cloister Walk

In search of a quiet religious ambience
Where he could reflect on divine benefactions,
Saint Anthony left his Lisbon friary,
Moving away from friends and family distractions.

In Coimbra he studied Scripture and the Fathers,
Committed reams to surefire memory.
His thoughts revolved around Divinity
While he consorted with saints in blissful colloquy.

He longed for martyrdom, but this was denied.
He sailed for Morocco to meet his destiny,
But illness laid him low and silent.
Later a storm tossed him to Italy.

God had not crammed him full of leaven
To waste it on a quick entrée into heaven.

The Collaboration

A shepherd girl saved her suffering land
From the oppressor's cruel and domineering hand.

Jealous of her gifts, they killed the child.
At nineteen she went, a frightened virgin mild.

They told the crowd she had done evil deeds.
The crowd held back so she could get her meeds.

Now down through the ages her reputation's grown
For God and France were the only loves she'd known.

The Collapsed Self

A glory shroud
      Life on the edge
            Descent into doggerel.

Communion

The swallows have returned from southern climes,
Scarce noticed in the busy wit of spring,
And daffy daffodils on sashay winds
Blow Your kisses to the saucy crowd.

I looked You up a branch of dogwood blooms
And caught Your wink in a sunlight peek on high.
You approached with a piece of humble bread
To veil our encounter from a stranger spy.

In Concert

All week I shuffle papers endless around
And on Sunday attend an arboretum recital.
The cello plays piano a mellifluent sound
While I drowse and let thoughts rumble vital.

Aphrodites fly from alliance to alliance,
Sampling nectar proffered to the surround.
Lilies bend in gracious compliance
While phlox stand straight all around.

A steadfast oak dapples light on the ground.
The concert done, my thoughts return at a scramble.
I greet old friends with courteous sound
And leave to others' ponder Nature's gambol.

A Conversation

Mignonne, allons voir si la rose
Qui ce matin avait déclose
Sa robe de pourpre au soleil,
A point perdu, cette vêprée,
Les plis de sa robe pourprée
Et son teint au vôtre pareil.

O Love, I quail to see the end of youth,
The coming end with somber ruth.
I pledge my life in Thy sweet race
To win for all Thy loving grace.
Look kindly on my daily place
With Thy full shining o'er-bent Face.

The Debut

Night descended soft upon the stage.
Heaven lay quiet on a Bethlehem hill.
Daylight folk shuffled to their rest.

A star transluced in the northern sky.
Angels choired as the play progressed,
And scenes unfolded before the invited guests.

Shepherds and wise men ushered by glory trace
Along inky aisles to their destined place
Adored of Light and Love the human face.

Decanting in Alcántara

Mystical prayer
        Abstracted air
                O earthly Paradise!

Wholly indifferent
        To crass emolument
                Rejoicing in sweet sorrow.

Rescuing guide
        From the great mudslide
                Into conventional debauchery.

He kept the beast from off the laity
By prayer and fasting and kindly charity.

December Friends

When the passing year sparkles snowflake white
And a Yule log flickers to chase away the gray,
We merrymake with conversation bright,
And in your eyes I see the love-light play.

I arrive for a Christmas visit with family and friend.
We meet amidst fragrant wreaths and Bethlehem song
And exchange thoughts and gifts and kisses at parties' end.
I see your joy, and the dream of love lives on.

I shy away from hollow, smiling men
That leave one stranded when one's most in need.
It's the inner light of love that excites my pen -
The light that drinks from heaven's mellow mead.

The thought of you in the morning calm
Is in all my days a faint-remembered balm.

Deciphering

In shuffle time the scramble circled
Until at last he puzzled to a halt.
"Where have you been?" the angels choired.

"The shepherds have come and gone,
The Bethlehem folk have all retired,
The star dissolved in morningtide.

"Where have you been?"
Wide-eyed, the scramble replied,
"At the crosswalks I was beguiled."

The Defense

Captious harpies discovered him alone,
Stomped a crevice in his soul.

Praying, knowing self-protect to no avail.

Divine wind blown, carping flown,
All restored in Deity.

The Defense of Poland, 1498

The Tartars and the Turks were in league,
And the plain folk of Poland shuddered.
An army of seventy thousand was fast approaching,
And panic seemed the most realistic response.

Then Ladislas of Gielniow, a Franciscan friar,
Counselled prayer as a defense.
Trust in God, he advised.

The people got down on their knees.
They prayed in their churches and in their bedchambers.
They prayed in their sackcloth, and in their pajamas,
In their Sunday best, and in their coveralls.

Then the wonder began. Two rivers overflowed.
Mother Nature wrapped the aggressor in icicles.
A blizzard turned living creatures into stone.
A remnant weathered the blast,
Only to be defeated by the Polish army.
Survivors vowed never to return to a country
Where the Defense was relying on acts of God.

Desert Thoughts in Autumn

We rambunctious assimilate
We do not control our plod.

Ego perishes
Among the autumn leaves.

We assault the earth
And the trees cry out revenge.

Make room for love
Under the eaves.

The storks fly away
And we pray for grace.

Love carries
Recalcitrant sheaves.

Destiny

"This soul is experiencing enough strains."
The shadows were discussing Emily.
She was shelved away in slower lanes
To live more privately.

Devil Trails

Devil trails in the brain end in pain.
These alien thoughts I took for my own.
I accepted ideas lacking in charity
And ratiocinated for a space
While you wandered alone in a separate sphere
And thought love was but a memory.
Then happily I discovered my mistake
And erased the blame with a contrition prayer.

Again I hear the laugh inside my soul,
The lap of eternity on my shores.
The ire and zany interpretations have disappeared.
I am not tricked by trapdoor subtleties
But have found my way back to love and laughter
And on clouds of prayer drift up to heavenly rafter.

The Dictator

He ascended on clouds of eloquence
And descended on thrusts of indigence.

The Director

For a wider stage he's left us.
We travel on in happy memory.
He once shook down anecdotes from heaven
To revive the embers of our childhood dreams.

Sir William's life was measured out in stories
Which he doled out in acting class
As suggested by his sainted mother
Whose intervention I divined in the end.

The Disenchanted

Now is the pining of our ancient strife
When cockles plant a wild and bitter fate
And winter breaks on friendship's warm relate.
Now is the sorrow of this mortal life.
I dreamt I would my brothers joyous greet.
I thought to find relations glad to aid
And friends to rally e'er the dream would fade,
But discover now a race for war unmeet.
Our mission they have failed to expedite,
The civil bond have severed and forsworn.
My vision was delusion thankless born,
The collective illusion ne'er so darkling bright.
I will set my gaze against the wayless sea
And in chartless desert live a hermit free.
No more of human destine will I dream
Nor seek my fellow in merry, jesting mood,
For I've a long, sad way to think and brood
And nights to watch before the dawn will gleam.
How many souls are lost to mortal love,
The light that quiet dawns within our eyes,
Since they stayed here to bed with shabby lies
And heeded not the summons from above?
So now the desert for my solitaire.
Hearken, my heart, no more to worldly trace,
But go where sin scars not our human face
And saints accept the Will of God in prayer.
There to faith and hope and love will I cling
And dip my thoughts in heaven remembering.

Disguises

So that none might revere Him out of fear,
Love came disguised in ragged effrontery,
As a child in oblivious Bethlehem
And a carpenter in rustic Galilee.

His marvelous light gave the blind their sight.
He left his friends a miraculous legacy
In an understatement of bread and wine
Before he sallied forth to sacrifice divine.

Distress

She wandered disconsolate from the flock
In her anxiety to be like everyone else.
At last God found her cowering in a cranny
And brought her home to feel the eternal pulse.

A Divine Romance

One patch of grey sky
Enhancing a few golden leaves
Seems no longer dull.
It lends a special beauty
To the warm glow of the lemon-shaded leaves.
So I, too, frame your exquisite charm
By perceiving its delicacy
And noting its particular excellence.
. . . . .
You stood there expectantly
Glancing about
The random crowd
As if to intercept
A special pair of eyes.

Minutes later I stole another peek.
You had forgotten your quest
In the delights of a laughing young girl.
Bitterly I reflected
On the fickleness of men.

But just then you walked toward me
In that idling crowd.
And the love-light
Flooding your dear eyes
Intently sought my response.

(12/4/1960)

Divine Union

In the wee hours of the night
Oliver Plunket bent over *The Imitation of Christ*.
His candle burned low as he read on.

"If ... you experience tribulation for the love of Christ
As a welcome, delightful gift,...
Then you have found heaven on earth." (2:12:6)

Thus he accessed the transports
Of divine union
And lavished them on his pastoring.

"So much as you are able
To go out of yourself,...
You will be united to God." (3:56:1)

After a lifetime of inserting love
In situations where it was missing,
He left the planet behind for a heavenly blessing.

Divinity Think

A Presence in the cosmos
    Looked down on Bethlehem.
An absence was desired;
    No midwife should attend.

A stable was selected
    Far from the haunts of men,
The midnight hour elected;
    No midwife would attend.

When Christ was born as was foretold
    At the empire's end,
Mary was in ecstasy;
    No midwife did attend.

Doubting Thomas Crisscrossed India

Down in the chaste and winnowing gauge of time
Where fortune's dilemmas sometimes force a choice,
There lived an innocent and careful man
Who went abroad in response to a heavenly voice.

Past feisty corsairs with their bristling points,
Past oriental despots jealous bold,
He steered his craft to South Asian lands
Where he labored hard to win a strategic hold.

Indeliberate he lived his life,
Full intent on watching the Designer's hand,
He followed dreams that others might have passed,
Preached the Truth where instinct ruled the land.

Nothing was too lean or spare for his sense
So mystical experience became a daily occurrence.

A Down Home Christmas

A star throw over midnight Bethlehem

An ambient spirituality
        And touch of merriment
           Love abroad

The chains of dross at a loss

The Doyenne of Society

She played at power games
Against the scrim civility.

Dreaming

When Joseph listened to an angel rhyme,
        He left convention behind
           And following that strange advice,
              Shattered the web of time.

Thrice he obeyed the angel voice
        Clear as a moonlight beam.
           He forsook his dark intelligence
              To rejoice in a heavenly dream.

The Dream of Love

The dream of love when wild men fought
And burghers grudged their due
Was frank beyond the ken of men
And oft bespoke untrue.

But prophecies of a virgin's child
In worldly Bethlehem
Were passed along from *père* to *fils*
Down the eclipse of centuries.

Then kindly Love sprang out the void
And merrily came to men.
The dream reached out to all alike
With its pleasures unalloyed.

The Dynamic of the West

I climbed the tower stair in the library
To the professor emeritus' literary lair
Where I found, surrounded by tome and manuscript,
Browsed a smiling, cherry-faced nondescript.

He welcomed me into his book-lined den
And launched a dictum, flourishing his pen.
"The West has gained in creativity
As its people have grown in spirituality.

"For two millennia the proportion of people
With personality and intellect has been rising.
A particular geography may regress,
But the general tendency is to progress.

"Prayer, ascetics, and kindly charity
Are spreading the reign of love in society.
Natural man moves on instinct and power,
But in the West love is in the place of honor."

We discussed the outcomes in technology
Of the ever more common urge toward charity.
Then after we with history did grapple,
I descended the stair and hastened to the chapel.

Earthbound

Kind pastors contemplate a world grown cold,
Silent 'neath the stars,
While their silly sheep drowse and browse.

A sudden light illuminates the scene.
An angel speaks in melody
While the silly sheep oblivious drowse and browse.

An angelic choir resounds o'er the shire.
The shepherd audience ascends a mystic stair
While their silly sheep oblivious drowse and browse.

Eden Revisited

Love looks not in silent introspect
But utters poetry to its love –
A stammering of happy eloquence,
A paradox arrayed in troubadour clothes,
A redundancy that frolics on a page,
A blessing loving and unique,
An elegance arrayed in choired Latin,
A prospect that renders men indifferent
To the vagaries of these our pilgrim days.

Embers

At dusk the autumn trees translate
          From russet flame to eidolon gloom.
I hurry to your hearth
          Clasping faint arrays of bloom.

To Emily

To everyone a hermitage
To which he can repair,
There to hold a converse,
There to say a prayer.

And if at first there is a pain
And life should scrape across the grain,
After comes a blessing time
When the soul will laugh in gentle rhyme.

Encounter by Jade Mountain

Pines drifted in the wind,
And snow flurried over the village.

Master Li laid aside his Analects
And sortied from the Pearl Cloud Pavilion
To survey the jade-flecked,
Snowy mountain cascade.

A maiden with a babe
Wrapped in her cloak
Crossed the philosopher's way.
Mother and child smiled a grace
And vanished from the glade.

They left nary a trace in the snow,
But Master Li folded away his Analects.
His thoughts were wrapped in ecstasy.

An Engineer Entrepreneur

My father was kind to children.
He spread out the funnies on the sunroom floor
And read to us from the adventures of Oaky Doaks
And the bumblings of Dagwood and Blondie.

He played with us in the yard:
Tag (we never could catch him),
Baseball, touch football, badminton
(He had an unbeatable ace).

He led me through the upper reaches
Of mathematics night after night.
I ascribed my A's totally to his tutoring.

He brought his papers home from the office
And worked on them at night and before dawn.
We saw this and always did our best in school.

He loved us. We never wondered about that.

The Eternal One

When in the twilight of a blustery afternoon
I think winter thoughts of grave philosophy,
Your laughter echoes in the halls of memory
And contradicts the pains of gravity.

I troll vast tomes for proofs and evidence.
I cast about for elusive counterrhyme.
Your love hovers expectant on the rim of the world
As I riffle the pages of rapscallion time.

At length I espy the haunts of the mystery
And trust the reports of immortality.
Your love will cancel death's grotesquery
When I step off the planet out of history.

The Extra-Terrestrial

God dreamt of a lad in a long-ago time
Who would run through the valleys of men
To unveil His love and decant a noble wine.
'Twas the fabulous tale that began in Bethlehem.

Fabled Waters

The Aegean laps iambic
Against a crumbling stone.
I splash my toes in its ripple.

The Fairy Fête

Mornings the sparkles descend.
The laugh is in the assembly glen,
And in this solemn time
The world is Paradise again.

Faithful to the Cross

When Christ was nailed to a Golgotha tree,
You and I were among the guilty pride
Of lions that looked on with incredulity.

He could have stopped the effrontery of the Cross,
But he chose to save the proud and the strong
From their souls' eternal loss.

Beneath the Cross sweet Mary and her cousin,
Contemplative John and the grief-struck Magdalen
Prayed to end this destiny inhuman.

Mary hung on, silently loving him.
He saw the brilliance of his mother's soul
And thought what might have been
Had Adam been more ascetic
And not bent to the serpent's end.

Fall Sowing

Unraveling memory
The clock ticks less in a hurry
Golden leaves flurry to the ground.

I tie memory knots
The clock returns to early sun
And night blots out the color clown.

In between the memory chores
I remember society swirls
While I plot networks of fresh capacity.

The Father

A winter moon floats over the mountains.
Orion hunts over the valley sleeping below.
Cassiopeia shimmers in radiant beauty
While Andromeda gleams in chains to see Perseus.
Unaware of this lantern world,
A father strolls pensively with his child.

"I have to leave you erelong.
I have to visit our ancestors forever,
And you must remain here yet a while.
I would go full of joy
If it were not for separating from you.
God calls me; I can hesitate no longer.
I will watch over your fate from above.
We will still be united
Until you, too, come into the everlasting light."

The world of the stars disappears with the dawn.
Orion no longer hunts over the valley.
Cassiopeia boasts of her beauty no more.
The constellations have fallen out of the sky.
Then the father unites with the light
And goes joyfully and transfigured into eternity.

A Faust Reverie

Helen, thy eye spoke love, thy voice a prayer.
Sweet rapture trembled on thy blushing brow.
I fell enthralled as thy most faithful knight
And undertook a solemn-vigilled vow.
Thy classic lines did prompt a flight of letters,
Epics and high tragedy have schooled.
Mere mortals have composed immortal lines,
By thy eye impressed and overruled.
Beauty, thy gaze translates my thoughts to heaven.
If eyes be windows of the immortal soul,
I would thy soul's guest full often be.
This crack in history all my senses stole.
I could toss away each elder logic book
And write fine paeans to thy loving look.

Fireflies

Little love lights
      sparkle in the night,
            entice
                  and confute the dark.

Random sprays of fireflies
      schedule their phosphor,
            winking a laugh
                  over a somber scape.

The sapient
      pacing earth-island
            select lambencies
                  to illumine a logic.

Capture one
      glowing on frequency,
            then, knowing, release -
                  another visibles.

Fireflies
      refract rhythmic glimpses,
            individual scintilla,
                  a moment.

The Fisher King

Love and rage reigned that day.
The sun glared down on blood and grime
While shops went in and out of business
In slow turnover time.

The fisher king was dragging a net.
Moneymen were wagging their heads
Over customer lethargy
While sadists were enjoying the spectacle.

Purgatory was contracting minute by minute.
The king had gone fishing,
Landing whales, clown fish
And presbyter males.

Flower Talk

How fair the day when flowers do hold court!
Here's a rose to murmur gentle love
That I your love remember gently by,
And here's a lily to trumpet the eternal Spring,
When all our woes shall lapse in memory,
And hyacinth to poesy the air,
As peonies our favorite haunts do share
And orchids laugh at playful breezes fair
And sing a song of love. See how the flowers
Intertwine their lives in graceful nooks
And crannies and before our sightless stare
For we little know and much dismiss
Their silent chatter. We have much to learn
From mere flowers had we the wit to know it.

The Forests of Carmel
In Memoriam Leonard Sandweiss

O'er the forest glades of wander-night Carmel
We toll the knell for dear departed friend,
Fresh embarked upon an ageless sea.
Where once he played upon the civic lyre,
Now fields lie silent beyond the fence of time.
The wind sifts moonflakes through the shrouded pine.
Crumbles centuries-soft a graveyard sign.

We thread through woods looking for tombs at night,
Query fools for subtle mortal ties.
The stars die out extinct in nebulae
While the moon dips in glossy mirror pools.
As we remember keen his righteous litigation,
In the woods resound the notes of threnody
That will after live a plaintive memory.

He was a member of the bar, fair and gentle-passioned,
A gentleman and a scholar, broad of mind.
With him departed the scrim civility.
So now we take to the forests of Carmel,
The flock that snuggles by a fire on a chilly eve.
Lamenting pipes the flute through mystic pines.
Silently praying throb fair angel lines.

Fountains Abbey

If loving were too subtle and refined
A thing for men to capture on the earth,
Then yon high stones have no tale to bind
Our hearts of thorn savaged in a mirthless birth.
Our forebears here in loving wise designed
To pass on to us an Olympian banquet spread,
A feast of bread and wine and song refined,
That we might find the gentle world not dead.
Now moss has gathered in the century cracks,
The song sits lost in a dusty file,
But the loving days of yore are faithful tracks
Where wondering pilgrims may wander yet a while.
These ruins once held a life so surpassing rare
That all our after-thoughts are golden fair.

"From their lairs"

From their lairs
The henchmen of Mephisto
Were catching people unawares.

Then the spirituality
Popped the imps off the planet
With fateful exorcism prayers.

A Frosty Night

On a frosty night
    In winter's blight
        A starry flight

Then Love looked out on the world.

Of Furies and Fairies

The Fury-driven snow fell to rage and splatter.
Oh, it had begun innocently enough –
A frosted dew, a rimy raindrop clatter,
Icicle shower and sashaying aster fluff.

I ventured out in wind-wet winter's veil
And sky-tossed wee folk crystal drop
While flakes of hail impaled my vest too frail
To the cascade of elfin snowball directed lop.

Then it clung to my face, nipped and snarled,
Lushed feather-wet through my castled hair,
Sliced with icy finger, silver-gnarled,
I ran distract to friendship circle lair.

I heard you laugh in anecdotal play
And prompt forgot the Furies' sharp mêlée.

A Gaelic Gala

Princess Marianne of Offaly
At one time held court with friends,
And ne'er was there a change in style
But she would set the trends.

She swept into her dappled gown
The night of the Offaly ball
And called upon her courtly friends
To meet her at the hall.

They came from out their coaches
To ascend the glittering stair.
They smiled and laughed right jollily
And were happy to be there.

They sang a cheery anthem
And fell to dish and ale
And danced until the morning
When the stars began to pale.

The princess called her favorite bard
And asked a song or two.
The bard replied he would oblige
And sang a medley true.

She called a trusted counselor
To try his wisdom bright,
And when he answered as a friend,
She honored him a knight.

At length the dance came to an end;
The friends they parted mellow,
And everyone thought they really ought
To sing for she's a jolly good fellow.

A Game of Chess

Baden-Baden glints with ancestral sophistication
As a concert ambles along to a conclusion.

We discuss Molière's joyous and sprightly rhyme.
"It was a simpler and perhaps a happier time."

You defeat the local champion
In a game of chess upon the hostelry lawn.

> A queen overtakes a king,
> While the peasantry circle a lonely rook.

You study abstruse scholarly reams
To buttress your hypotheses and your dreams.

We sit beneath an umbrella and admire
A summer flounce and her ruddy squire.

We discuss Monet and his bright impressions
While your eyes transluce in pale blue digressions.

> Knights advance on a king
> Scant guarded by a lowly pawn.

"You have a happy heart."
"I am happy but apart."

We wander under dismal mountain pine
Where shadows trace a melancholy line.

I remark your gravity and happiness blend
And breathless watch your gentle soul unbend.

> A bishop reduces a castle
> And approaches the redoubted queen.

No one is around to observe our shadowbox trail
As love slow unveils the Holy Grail.

We listen to a yodel on an edelweiss knoll.
You look into my smiling soul.

You suggest that to be worldly wise and profound
One must trod where love and faith abound.

> A rook advances down an open aisle
> To within striking distance of the queen.

The heavens shimmer blue and dazzling white.
In your eyes shines an immortal light.

"Perhaps love lies in self-abandonment
And the acquisition of a starry referent."

You bend down for a heavenly kiss;
I float in the sky beyond all mortal bliss.

> On my finger shines a blessing ring.
> King and queen in happy ever aftering.

The Garret

Under the eaves
> Your love I remember -
>> Golden interventions
>>> In dolorous November.

The General

Helmeted and brash, the general rode to the ramparts.
After surged the men and stormed and won.
Late the general retired full of plans,
Prayed the field to win when next the sun.

Again the general spurred the men into battle.
Everywhere rose the hopes of embattled France.
The general pressed on, the men grew bold and strong,
Then the foreign foe fled before their lance.

Sunday came to rescue the hapless invader.
The general desisted and from the fray withdrew
For quiet time and strategy and prayer
For unto God the victory was due.

Then one day ta'en amidst a battle whirl,
The visor raised, they found, afaint, a girl.

Georgetown

Alma Mater, your gray, imposing spires
Ascend the sky on cloud retreats to God.
Where scholars light their civilizing fires,
After midnight John Carroll walks the Quad.

Alma Mater, your light illuminates
Freedom's renaissance on pilgrim sod.
Where courage plants and philosophy meditates,
After midnight John Carroll walks the Quad.

Alma Mater, you offer friendship fair,
And on your paths both North and South have trod.
Where the dynamic of our race we weld and share,
After midnight John Carroll walks the Quad.

Docent and counselor to a nation's rise,
Alma Mater, clarion and wise!

The Ghost of Dublin

In gray urbane I strayed a quayside lane
      While shutters slept along the daedal dawn.
In the dim I espied a frayed and shaggy shade
      To which I was sudden circles drawn.

Cloud towers radiant in an Angelus chime
      Announced the triumph of a moon-fade sky.
The shade sped light on fainting, breathless tread,
      Fled deserted streets on a rosy high.

It hastened breathless through St. Stephen's Green,
      Then lingered round the halls of Belvedere.
When I thought to grasp it by the College chapel,
      It evanesced in sunlight melting screen.

A wind cried haunting soft against my ear,
Ireland, how could I leave you yesteryear!

Glendalough

The monks are gone, and the vale lies painterly still,
Strayed into ruins where chancelled saints and scholars.
The round tower watches o'er the dell
With few to listen to the tales its ports would tell.

"God listens the world"

God listens the world
Children playing round
And from time to time He speaks.

Golden Fluffy

A girl of three
Walks around experimenting
Tasting, touching, sensing
Navigating islands of tables, sofas, chairs
Situated in air-space.

Blonde waves hazing round her face
She taps, opens, inserts, presses
Memorizing motion
And recording its consequences
As a scientist in his work space.

But most of her waking time
Is spent in conversation
Making us merry
While she moves about
Securing ideational space.

"Goldfish in a mirror pond"

Goldfish in a mirror pond
Await boat drift to know direction.
I follow love.

Gracemere
A Private School for Girls

I remember an old Victorian manse
Set on an oak lawn knoll
Where we scrambled down the servants' stair
In humble freshman role.

Marie Vénard beamed us lakes of grace
While Mary Jonathan scholasticized
On the freedom of the Nichomachean race.

Mary Bertrand interspersed our English rhymes
With stories of her childhood friends
And their inimitable shenanigans.

Helen Mary announced our paltry chemical worth
While Mary de Paul allowed a French Noël
Escorting angels to the holy birth.

Mary Dunstan predicted we would prefer nonfiction
While Mary Alice taught the compromise
Of many a statesman turned mathematician.

John Francis faciled the research of bibliophiles
And scrambled us over algebraic paradigms,
Mustering us through Euclid's geometric trials.

G. Marston Haddock directed our plays and pageants
And rehearsed in Broadway melodies our choir
For the flowery Daughters of the British Empire.

Yet of all laetitious memories
I most fond and fast recall
How you charmed our afternoons 'twixt two and three
With tales of loving children's mischievery.

Gracemont

O my little soul
Lost on a wild atoll
      Solitudes of grace.

The Grandmother Nuns

Nesting in pews, chapelling a prayer
Paging the Scripture to frequent a phrase
A sister passes, triumph of angels
Resting from half a century of children souls
In gentle retirement from the roustabout world
Homeward bound.

The Great Wall

A thousand-mile wall in mountains cresting
Watches on against barbarian attacks.
It lies athwart the tentatives of power
And fends off the foreign devil's ax.

A thousand-mile wall defends the dwellings of love
And guards the wisdom of the centuries.
Posted here and there are sentinels
Lest alien hordes attack our rhapsodies.

Harvard Days

In Cambridge lairs we fared on patient pages
Where rambled English lights and Rhenish sages.

We dreamt of Renaissance and French festoons,
Follied in a teashop afternoons.

We mused with tutors by forgotten embers
And sherried merry dons in gray Decembers.

They read the prophetic content of the past
And taught the practice of this sovereign last.

In oratories and historic bays
We conversed with peers in quiet after plays.

We warmed to rivals in our football quarrels
And sculling crews that chased the royal Charles.

Yet a question lingered, dearest friend.
Faint the answer in midnight light a blend.

The Hay Child

He slumbered in a manger drear,
In country ways a slum,
With pokes of straw around his head,
The world beneath his thumb.

Wise pastors and kind sapients
Were prompt to holy trace.
A child looked out his lowly bed,
All heaven in his face.

The Hermit Poet

He visited the source –
Dried to a pucker.
He retreated within the borders of the mind –
Unpeopled with thoughts.
He searched the libraries of his ambience,
The shelves of established rhyme,
Troubled classic prose with a tired finger,
Wrenched his ears after anecdotes,
Practiced incongruity,
Walked in paradox,
Fell silent before his audience.
He found nothing of merit to say,
No banter, no proverbs,
No cliché or case imaginative.
His mind fell into prose
And all the gates thereof did close.

A Highland Memory

When I think on the mists of Scotland
And on her sunlit bays,
I remember all the happiness
Of those more youthful days.

We went into the mountains
And danced the Highland fling.
We tossed the mighty caber
And joined in communal sing.

The lads were sharp, the lassies green.
The children all were mellow.
The burghers told their stories old,
And everyone loved his fellow.

So when all the clans are gathered
At the ending of our life,
There'll be a bagpipe skirling
And kilts beyond the strife.

Hilarius

Much had I read in Roman times
Of scholars in their sundry realm.
Depressed in Plato's shadow cave,
I longed for a more certain helm.

My studies brought me home to God.
On Him I made my meditate,
Forsook my friends in a remnant creed,
And embraced the Faith illuminate.

And when I plucked me out the crowd
And followed fairest charity,
I found I gained in cheery throng,
Immersed in fine hilarity.

The people saw me in my joy,
Selected me for bishop's seat.
I thought to find the hand of God
Sifting through the fine-blown wheat.

I gave me o'er to God alone;
With material goods I left my wife.
Then through the balm of holy oil
I was freed from worldly strife.

The emperor came an Arian blind
And asked me for a nod.
I loved my Faith to this extreme –
I left my native sod.

He exiled me to Phrygia.
While there I made research
And wrote some reams upon my love
That steaded up the Church.

I converted many a Grecian friend
So they sent me home to Gaul
Where I blithely praised the Lord all day
And smiled on heaven's call.

The Holly Boy

I walked upon a wintry path,
Plucked holly on the way.
The wind blew sharply to deter
My joy on Christmas Day.

Then saw I a tiny child
Who lay smiling on the ground.
When I stopped to view this wonder,
'Twas a heavenly babe I found.

His kindly look struck me amaze;
I thrilled to see his face.
I vowed him all my simple gain,
Found in his plan my place.

Homo Sapiens

He raised his head from scholars' squabbles
And disdained the conversational rubble
To notice the redemption.

A God-Man passed the moats of Hades
From Bethlehem to Calvary
And won him an exemption.

He thought he might reciprocate
And joyfully work an apostolate
With the Beloved his lasting contemplate.

The Honey Song

When by the lost compass of the moon I sped
And fled the heady wine of music fair
To seek a respite from all worldly dread,
I raptured watched with God a vigil prayer
And felt there then no strain against the throng.
No ghostly fingers to tap my brain and try
Its overthrow, but recaptured the honey song
And heard its dulcet note by God on high.
Do you seek to make a changeling heart
And finger fast a brain to chart its course
When I by tradition bound am loath to start
On wandering, having reveled in the source?
Come share with me the honey song of love
And seek no more my immortal soul to shove.

Inn of the Lost Pilgrim

Chopsticks all a-twaddle,
I cannot hear your heart.

The International Society

English grammar and rich confabulation
Fly around in a verbal cannonade.
Dons who live on eldering memory
Marshal words in magnanimous parade.
Dictionaries flap to a conclusion
And French and Latin fresh ideas beget
As we joust along in conviviality
And ne'er good fellowship will forget.
Our love and wit and forthright gallantry
Will but younger be in blithe eternity.

Investments and a Dividend

John Capistrano became a mad investor,
Sacrificing to folly for Christianity.
Sleep, food and ego predilections
He tossed aside to fight inanity.

John campaigned in Italy and Central Europe.
With miracles he buttressed his argument.
He spoke to the crowds through an interpreter
And convinced the people to obey the covenant.

When in old age he faced the Sultan at Belgrade,
The countryside rallied to aid this prodigy.
Armed with pitchforks and household cutlery,
They learned from him a spiritual strategy.

The janissaries began their assault after dark,
Advanced relentless o'er the city walls.
The Hungarian general withdrew his garrison.
The townsfolk followed in pyjamas and hasty shawls.

John prayed up a storm in the citadel.
His raw recruits let loose a bramble fire
That rolled downhill on the doughty janissaries
And turned the field into a hellish mire.

The defenders thus snatched victory from defeat.
The Sultan retreated with sobering casualty.
John had harvested a dividend,
But the credit was shared with chary Hungary.

Ireland Abroad

God sent the dreamy Irish
Across the emerald bay
To found a royal empire,
To say an ancient pray.

They sailed to far Iona
And on to Lindisfarne.
They walked to farthest Germany
And prayed at every tarn.

God sent the merry Irish
From out their native shire
To spread the love of laughter,
To light a Celtic fire.

Fresh continents they traveled,
Shared in the modern age,
But ne'er forgot tradition
And loved their heritage.

So when they all are gathered
In heaven at the last,
There'll be a light regaling
With all their memories past.

Isaiah's Child

From the round corners of blithe eternity
Into the hollow chains of contemporaneity
Slipped a heavenly Babe in swaddling clothes disguised,
Prophesied to make wise men foolish and foolish men wise.

"I wandered through the city sere"

I wandered through the city sere,
Lonely as the night drew near,
Until I met you, fine and dear,
And settled by your hearthside shy.

You took me in, a needy fellow.
I drank the mead of friendship mellow,
And all about did welcome bellow
As we passed our cheer from heart to heart.

You held me close in laughing eye
And touched repose in stranger sky,
O'erleapt the choice of ego vie
To share the counterpoint of love.

I will always think you heaven-sent
As you my life sweet grace have lent.

John Paul II

He wore patched knickers from provincial Poland
Under the ceremonial robes of the papacy
To demonstrate his nothingness before God.

No friend or adversary could detect an ego
Since he never defended himself or sought to impress.
He was not himself, but another Christ.

While mannered men wreaked havoc in little ways,
He walked the world accessing grace –
A priest in rags beneath the pageantry.

Joseph

He listened to angels in dreams
And lived in union with God.
He led a happy life,
Levitating above the sod.

He was a kindly man,
Honest to his core.
He married above his station;
His son he had to adore.

But in his dying days
He knew the joy of grace.
He had trodden the plod of God
And left for a heavenly place.

Julian

O good divine favor, O loving blessed
     That melts into my flesh a union
Under form conventional our communion.
     They scatter to their rackets unimpressed.

You come in lilies to a mystic space
     And drift along a pomegranate bend.
You watch every tumbledown I tend.
     They play at matches unaware of grace.

I fly away on whim and search for more,
     To be the love you cherish most on earth.
I ponder your sweet and melancholy mirth.
     They ratchet up a dusty, shabby score.

All will be well and all will yet be well
So long with love I humble, faithful dwell.

The Junior Partner

At Crumpety, O'Shayne & Edwards
I became learnèd in my profession.
I worked on high finance
In many a midnight session.

I learned the trade from Jim
Who remembered every cue.
I modeled all my conduct
On his more practiced view.

A dozen years have passed
Since I've followed in his shoe
From assistant through to manager
And now as partner too.

So, friends, let's all be cheery
For good fellows they are rare,
And let our bonds ne'er wither,
But each shall do his share.

For life is in the living.
Fine fellows have their day.
And when we pull together,
All troubles fade away.

So let's hearty for each other
And never look askance
To ask if one's a brother
Or if to take a chance.

If success is to the giving,
And gain is to the friend,
Let's ride the crest together
And find the rainbow's end.

Kimono Moon

A teacup drifts imprecisely
      Along a koto note
            And paper walls slide awry the sky
                  You descend to pillow talk

Light falling through the lattice leaves.

Kimono Snow

Snow silently cloaks the trees,
      And I in my library
            Ramble on a story trail.

Quietly falls the snow.
      A lady walks on sandal foot,
            A child within her sleeve.

I rise to beckon her in,
      And the sun comes out
            Warm and inviting.

Kinesis

The ascetic soul climbs up with joy to God.
      Abandoning the ash of history,
           The soul finds its home
                In bright Divinity.

Lady of Clairvaux

When sunset bathes gray cloister stones in gold,
And monks retire each to private prayer,
Then Mary watches with her merciful Son
And graces dreams that ascend the heavenly stair.

For the maiden who mothers her flock with clemency
Bernard vigiled, reciting the Memorare,
Imploring this living Scripture to grant his prayer
To erase the fate that menaced the random starry.

Mary once counseled women in Galilee,
Listened to their griefs and sought a remedy.
She was chef and seamstress to the followers of the Lord
And prayed to rearrange their destiny.

She shared in the suffering of Calvary
And intercedes now for earthbound peasantry.

The Lady of the Lake

I wandered bemused in a hickory wood
On a path edged with violets astray
When in my way there stepped a bonny lass
Robed in the scarlets of unending day.

She counseled me to listen carefully
To every thought of my sovereign lord.
She led me to a lake so blue serene,
Showed a stone whence sprang a knightly sword.

I knelt and pledged my heart in faithful vow
To atone for wrong and measure up to grace.
I asked for pardon and the strength to grasp
Excalibur in strong and fond embrace.

Lake Chartreuse

A lake transluced in a solitary dream
Reflecting shards of starry marigold fire.
I felt Your touch reach out from valley spire
As the moon lapped down in shimmering aster stream.

You murmured gently in my heart with charm
As ganders startled from a moonlit park.
I strolled a-courting in the hushèd dark.
You whispered soft to stay all sense of alarm.

The night was full of faith and saving grace.
The moon illumined from an invisible sun.
Into Your arms did I so gladly run,
Detached and chased from senseless passion's race.

I broached the lake in lilting, loving sail,
Banished from all luckless, craven quail.

Lament

God! Would that I had not offended
Your trove of unheeded wisdom
Your heart of unkissed love
Your side of forgotten mercy
Your hands of unwanted suffering
Your feet of disregarded obedience
Your lacerated back of unconsidered humility.

The anguish in your eyes
Pierces my neglected soul
To see the darkling filth
I would instantly disown
To watch Your secret smile.

(1960)

Laurels

Of friendship in antique Roman day
Men thought with it nothing did compare.

"Nihil cum amicitia illius possum comparare."

Virtue made friends, they loved to say.
Good men make friendship passing fair.

"Virtus tua me amicum tibi facit."

A tranquil mind, strength, prudent simplicity, friends –
These make up the life of the blessed.

"Mens quieta, vires, prudens simplicitas, amici –
haec vitam beatiorem faciunt, iucundissime amice."

And yet they knew a man must be alone
To find the soul that shines in company.

"Animus se ipse alit."

A learnèd man has thoughts to hone;
His inner delights are many.

"Homo doctus in se semper divitias habet."

We do not succeed by physical strength or agility
But by wisdom, eloquence and ability.

"Non viribus et celeritate corporum magna gerimus,
Sed sapientiae et sententia et arte."

Lawrence of Arabia

Those summers spent a country lance
Cycling Crusader castles and their towns,
Buoyant in conversation with village France,
He learned more than taught the chary Oxford gowns.

Those summers spent hardy and on the roam
Frank established the strategic mode.
He flung defiance at the bournes of home,
Absorbed the practice of the knightly code.

And while the psyche birthed and grew apace,
He wined on the poesy of Old Provence
And fabulous Table Round and courtly ways
And spent a memorable night in abbey haunts.

Yet he lingered a hostage to his dam –
An ascetic soul in spiritual bedlam.

The Legacy

In the morning of the world
A young couple traveled
Along the road to Bethlehem.
The air was chill and still,
Muffled the monotonous plod.

As humble folk they fared along,
Forgotten in the somber throng.
They kept up their spirits when all was wrong.
The maid was rapt in contemplation,
Her child waiting to be born.

That night on a hideaway hill,
In a shelter for rude beasts,
She birthed unknown a royalty.
Some shepherds pledged their loyalty,
And days later wise men knelt in awe.

From their obedience great Love was born
And fruitful dwelt in the land.
They themselves found joy
In making a space on earth for Divinity,
Thus enabling what planned the Trinity.

The Letter Child

You and I exchanged notes
Across a choppy economic sea.
After a long hiatus we repast,
Two exiles on a sudden free.

They are listening to our love,
Chopsticks idle at another table,
As dewdrop voices brush the dust
From off an ancient and fantastic fable.

You bend forward to reverent clasp
What never left my sure and loving grasp.
Your eyes light up with smiles
That compensate the weary teardrop trials.

Levitating

Threnodies of time
        Are lost in the labyrinths of Latin.
Mourning turns into glory –
        Cushions of air in angel space.

At length I understood
        The science of the saints.
When Newton became an ascetic,
        He fathomed earthly constraints.

Lightning

Karol Wojtyla was about to give a sermon.
The congregation was expectant
But perhaps not totally receptive.
Then the lightning began, and he winced.
When it was over, he mounted the pulpit
And gave a homily that spoke to men's hearts.

"Little valentines dropped out the sky"

Little valentines dropped out the sky
And nestled in cold winter's empty spaces.
I found myself in the Divine Eye
Which reinterpreted the somber places.

Living Above the Natural Level

My mother became an ascetic after her cancer operation.
Following the nutritional guidelines given her by Providence,
She changed from recreational dining in restaurants
To meals at home with a view to abstinence.

When she moved to a Franciscan residence,
She stipulated half-portions in the dining room
And waved away desserts afloat in whipped cream insouciance.

She eschewed the folly of bingo and romantic movies
And in the chapel reviewed her Scriptural memories.

In the end she even gave up her preprandial shot of brandy.

A Loft

I live a sparrow midst the burghers
Of this Sleepy Hollow town,
A throw from all the happy shout
Of the bustling city clown.

My hermitage sits an aeyrie
Betwixt the earth and sky
While around the tree kind children
Play merrily to my spy.

The Lord of History

Born into a time when Rome ruled the world
And Athens reigned in letters and philosophy,
A Child-God in backwater Bethlehem
Lay wrapped against the danger of a chill.

He saw a mother redolent with wonder,
An army of angels with the shepherds they advised,
And astrologers who divined the significance
Of a wandering star and followed it afar.

The Child smiled on his constituency.
Time would lend it weight and gravity.

The Lost Thought

A thought settled out of sight
Among some abandoned leaves.
I wanted to retrieve it
And searched among the sheaves.

I thought I saw it on a shelf
In staves concerning love,
But then it swirled and hid away
In realms more high above.

Often when I sudden wake
Upon a midnight long,
I think I hear that thought again,
A thrush in quiet song.

The Lost Wedding

A petal floats on invisible eddies earthward.
Soon its fellows queuing for dismissal
Waft bridal white beneath our feet.

When all her boughs their radiant veil have lost
And only jade globes append,
Lo! Two moons harvest jacinth fruit.

Now snowflower lace is but a memory blurred.
Gently, sadly, she watches others labor
As she rushes standing to her fate.

The Love Insurrection

Into the miasma of a pagan world
Leapt Eternal Love.

Where instinct and power rudely ruled the day,
Now smiled a manger Babe.

The throne discovered this untimely insurrection
To its eminent dismay.

It deployed blind troops and worldly sycophants
To slay the innocent.

A family hastened to a neighbor land
Where Love in peace could stay.

Love in the Desert

A wrinkle sat a rift in his expression,
Of anxious thoughts the sad and dour confession.

His hair was clumped in graying antique scrolls
Around a face with dead men's eyes for holes.

His growling voice was cracked from yield to bad
And groped for phrases through a length of sad.

Into this desert I wandered unaware,
A fairy child before his wondering stare.

The Love Project

When the world was grey and living in travesty,
Out the Eternal Sun dropped the Eternal One
To visit the catastrophe
For its instruction.

The Lover

Joyous maples
      Float in the wind.
I go over my lessons,
      Little distracted by your slow love.

"Love spoke out in ancient Palestine"

Love spoke out in ancient Palestine
And miracles worked to give the world a sign.
Then it sped along the arteries of Rome
To dwell in hearts a sovereign divine.

Love's Strategy

Snow clustering soft
      Baby cradled in a stable
            Round-eyed mother's watch

Hark! An angel sings.

"Love was born in Bethlehem"

Love was born in Bethlehem
      On a whisper of the night.
           It filtered through the centuries,
                A slowly gathering light.

Low Tide

The saints are not so visible
In sunny times
But are lights in the darkness
When nothing rhymes.

Men let go their moorings
And friendship ends in derision.
Nothing's wrong and nothing's right,
And the only discouragement is prison.

Loyola

En una noche oscura,
Con ansias en amores inflamada,
¡Oh dichosa ventura!
Salí sin ser notada,
Estando ya mi casa sosegada.

Gazing past the stonebread dam
And clambering out the wine-dark sod,
Oh delightful adventure!
I evaded all their capture
And entered into God.

Lucubrations

Meditating on a fragment of memory,
He examined the trajectory
Of the woman selected by God.

Mother of fair love,
    Mother of my soul,
        Ark in which we evade shipwreck,
            Solace of our wandering,
                Fighter for those who trust in you.

Show yourself a mother.

He was hoping for a vision mild
But slept when the dawn exploded in fireworks
And in the shadows a maiden smiled.

Lullaby Lake

Under the rafters
    Float our laughters
        Stories from the past
            Masks that do not last.

Hideaway games
    Memory flames
        Trapdoor attic play
            To chase away the senseless gray.

Lullaby Sky

The angels attended, choir on choir.
Dreamy-eyed cherubim and morning seraphs
Caroled on a midnight hill.

A narrow rook they lullabied,
Drifting in and out,
Consoling a heavenly child
Awake to a rude world.

Lullaby Wind

Lullaby wind
     Snow gentle
          Light leaps down to cradle
              God within.

The Madonna Painting

Crossing through the Renaissance Salon
On my way to the Kandinsky Gallery,
I am arrested by a pale blue
Cloaking a woman's form.
It is a Fra Lippo Lippi tableau
Of the Nazareth bride
Who consented to God's enterprise.

So Love was born in tumbledown hostelry!

Mapling in the North Country

I remember mapling time in the Maine woods
When the snow lay mounds in velvet sheet
And our boots crunched thick and icicles popped
And fallen boughs crackled loud beneath our feet.
I snuggled warm in my muskrat hood.

I remember Old Jeff would get out a pail
And fix his drill and tap into the sap,
And the tree gave forth its honey lode.
So watched I rapt its gentle lap,
An amber flow that did not fail.

Now I live in the city and the closest
I get to a sap-filled maple tree
Is lumps of figured sugar in a department store,
But I remember the life of the tree
And how it always gave its best.

To Mary

From the onward march of unrelenting time
I note I cannot a single day recall
To retrogress or prove I was in rhyme
With the divine love that holds us all in thrall.

I think on you who to the Eternal prays
And on your beauty that the eye enchants.
Your charms show to heaven joyful ways,
And in your voice the dearest love decants.

Then from all rue I swift and glad rebound.
If your melodious voice makes such earthly joy,
Then death's approach makes a less unhappy sound.
So your sweet love all menace does alloy.

Inevitable death may come with somber tread,
But your loving heart restores me from all dread.

Mater Orphanorum

A verity perdures from antique Latin days,
That for souls who wobble in this dolorous maze
There cares a mother in the sky.

Mellifont

When sunset etches quiet in the glen,
And shadows fret across the whispering land,
The stones tell silently of the heavenly leaven,
And memories rush o'er the forest stand.
These forsaken ruins at one time sheltered
A font of honey for the neighboring land.
Then chanting made men strong and gentle spurred
And spoke of loving fine and rapture grand.
In those days larks lofted high
And soared into the moonlight on the rand.
Once clouds wandered in the sky
O'er trysts with God on this now deserted land.
These ruins to hope the despairing twilight spanned.
Our daylight dreams seem shadows and less grand.

Memories of a Country Childhood

Canoe Brook

A spring has grown civilized on our land.
Grandmother has planted careful terraces
That slope down to a tadpole pool.
Miniature mosses and May flowers cluster behind pebbles
While froglets splash careless in the sun
And waterflies skate a zigzag path.
Father has split logs
To make a stairway down to the bridge
From where the brook jags away into the wild.

The Visit

We visit friends at their cottage in the woods.
An enormous Christmas tree lights up the high ceiling
And candles illumine lattice bays.
There is social conversation
And the passing of gingerbread cookies.
The children watch cowboy movies;
The white hats are the good guys.
We love the house because it is old
And resembles the cottage where the dwarfs lived.
The afternoon sun lapses quietly
So we kiss both cheeks goodbye
And depart that enchanted cot.

Spruce Mountain

Once you and I light caroused the day,
Nudging pucks into pockets
And leisuring over jigsaw puzzles.
Evenings we danced to a fiddle with the local gentility
And learned the Virginia reel,
To do-si-do and sashay.

I remember a hayride in the soft September night
When we listened to country songs
And a guitar that catered to every request.
Mornings we rambled mountain trails
To pluck blackberries
And in the afternoon we backstroked
In a dappled pond.

Blueberry Island

Once more you and I row across the lagoon
To visit our solitary island
Where we fantasy Peter Pan and Wendy.
We clamber over rocks in search of the Lost Boys
And hide in blueberry crannies
From pirates on the prowl.
The sun gently warms our imagine
As we play free and happy
Until the bell summons us to the mainland again.

Envoi

This idyll we shared in coinciding time
When heaven shone down upon the gracing lea.
Still in the memory does it happily chime
As close we walk to bright eternity.

Merry Ireland

The Irish are a-laughing.
They are so bold and mellow.
Their eyes they are a-sparkling,
And hearty is each fellow.

An Irish love's forever
And is of earth the leaven
Since Patrick chased away the snakes
And made their isle a heaven.

The Microdot Worm

Like the vile worm,
Indiscernible from a splinter
Save for its directional,
So I in the sight of the Creator
Am easily extinguished.

Yet loved
And besought to love.

Midnight Tryst

Snowflakes laze across an inky trail.
   I pick my way from out the crofty hills.
      In Bethlehem a dreamy laughter Boy!

Migrations

A poem locked in language
Collapses in translation.

Usually in the reinvention
Some of the brilliants
Fall off.

My Mind a Rookery

When deceptive pleasure grounded out
      And prayer immersed a scripted rookery,
Swift into the dark abyss of time
      Leapt light and love and mystery,
And fractures of anathema
      Collapsed in the dust of history.

Mingling

The sun sank past our jaded joys
As we played at fripperies
In an autumn cabaret.
The trees hung golden, flush and frozen
In the cold, grey sky, and the stars
Stayed silent out of sight
Though we knew their whereabouts.

There was a poet who came to the language
Through a rustic Anglo-Saxon.
Another learned to speak with Latin intellection,
And yet another talked with Greek accoutrement
While I gravitated to a French nuance.

We conversed along certain tested spoors.
You digressed on periwinkle shells
While I proffered Rembrandt with a twinkling eye.

Your sword tongue turned to butter knife.
Else would you have skewered yourself
In slicing me.

The resort was nearly deserted
And all our summer friends homeward flown
As the golden leaves were lightly blown
Past the face of a curious moon.

A Miscalculation

When he traveled out of human history,
He left no trace in dilettante memory.
His chance to love had sadly gone awry.
He asked the Almighty for pardon with a sigh.

Mist

The mist billowed off the River Styx
And engulfed a valley of men.
It shrouded sturdy oak and graceful ash
So that the ghosts of past and future vanished
And only the narrow present remained.

The mist o'erpowered drowsy flowers
That nodded in their quiet bowers.
It prowled through haystack meadows
Searching for a maverick owl
To beguile with a crackerjack lie.

The mist tried to o'erleap the mountains
To cover other dells
But could not.
It cowered before our friendly bastion.

Moments

Not the trivia is squirreled away in memory
Nor the shadows scratching on my windowpane,
Hoping to gain entrance,
But … the ecstasy.

The Moonflower

When dreams drift down the terraced clouds of air
And quiet plies a constellation by,
Claire pauses on a cold and stony stair
And breathes kind thoughts to the expectant sky.

She basks attendant on a light divine
And dances in the universal flow
Of sparks that upward fly from the angel wine
And bread that seek a gentle overthrow.

The dawn is breaking, and Claire in union rare
Revels in an oceanic love.
Matins bells arouse her from her prayer.
Swift departs the bright and kindly dove.

O Claire, espoused to Beauty ever ancient and new,
Grant this thy sight to our more feeble view.

Morning Trail

Spring beauties open pearly white
Their cups to catch the morning dew,
And I, breathless at the lovely sight,
Forget my tale of wild and somber rue.

For I in jungle glare have grown,
Scratched by thistle and by thorn.
Woeful winds have me full measure blown.
I joy forgot, all fragile and forlorn.

Yet flower grails do yield fair promise
To those who look for sights unknown
For beauty lives on when all's amiss
In seeds of love and life eternal sown.

In a Mountain Valley

In a high mountain valley I ventured out
  Upon a day so daisy-fresh at dawn,
Beheaded dandelions in the lawn,
  Sang blithe rounds to robins at their rout.

You strolled among the edelweiss so bright
  And spoke of trust to those in slavery.
I surrendered to your love so marvelous free
  And communed with you in soft and nimbus light.

You fathomed secrets I had grown to fear
  And planted every saving grace and call.
You smiled to see me rapture heaven's thrall
  And dried away each restless human tear.

O Love, I love with all I hold most dear
For loving is my life, my hope, my cheer.

The Music Lover

When the social whirlwind ebbed and flowed away,
And an unfriendly spirit whispered despondently in her brain,
Jeanne had recourse to the happy sounds of music,
And these tended to the religious vein.

She attended choir concerts and musicals
And memorized the prayer group repertoire.
The choir Mass on Sundays raised her to heaven,
And classical music wafted through her boudoir.

During her year in the Franciscan residence
Jeanne enjoyed listening to the chapel carillon.
She danced to zumba music in exercise class
And attended recitals in the common.

For her joyous farewell to this unhappy planet
Jeanne chose some music that altered her throes.
The celebration began with *Lift High the Cross*,
A reminder that Christ himself shared our woes.

Then she honored Our Lady with an *Ave Maria*.
At communion time the *Panis Angelicus* meditate
Resounded in an atmosphere of loving contemplate.
Therefore the Redeemed closed reflection on man's eternal fate.

And at the cemetery she serenaded
The disconsolate throng with a cardinal's song.

The National Birthday

In the morning we attend a village parade.
People sing anthems with stanzas blurred.
Young girls wave by on fancy floats
While the mayoralty sweeps along chauffeured.

In the afternoon we join in children's games,
Tossing raw eggs in ever widening arcs
And racing with our feet in a burlap bag.
We chase a greased watermelon in swimming larks.

After dark we gather on the esplanade
To watch fireworks shot from a storied isle.
The night is mild, and we are caught agape
At every flower shower sparkle's wile.

And when the stars display their lanterns fair,
We lift our hearts in humble, thankful prayer.

The Nightingale Floor

The courtiers bow to me all the day long,
Walking to and fro over the nightingale floor
Which chirps under their slippers.

We sip tea and calculate
How many lords and their retainers
Will bring tribute in the coming year.
We pick over rice cakes with our chopsticks
And discuss the harvest and country business.
The courtiers bow very low
And politely come and go.
They carry messages across the moat
Where carp dawdle, idly passing the day
While we are so busy.
The ladies throw tidbits to the carp
And flash their fans.

In the evening they bring us raw fish
And make light conversation.
A poet reads some haiku,
And a Zen master tells us puzzling stories.

Finally, we wish to retire for the night.
The courtiers depart over the moat,
And the servants withdraw after many bows.

My wife nods drowsy on her mat
While I lie awake
Listening for the nightingale.

Nights

Idle and alone in the watches of the night,
He lost his aplomb and stumbled toward despair.
Too much rest in the arms of Morpheus
Was threatening him with a Stygian repair.

Attributing his plight to lethargy,
He searched in books for an analogy.
He knew sluggish ways were doomed to fail,
And all would come to a bitter wail.

Then he remembered of yesteryear a tale
And thought its application could not fail.
Saint Catherine of Bologna did not quail
But vowed to persist till heaven's intervention.

Catherine escaped insidious Morpheus' charms
By praying in the night with generous outstretched arms.

The Night Watch

They clustered in a field afar.
The lambs lay close to their mothers warm.
The shepherds listened the night to hear
The prowl of wolves in a swarm.

The night was dim with snow suggest.
The moon was locked in a luster cloud.
The pastureland with lambs a-drowse
Was far from royal banquets proud.

A glory shone on a quiet high.
An angel spoke the words of joy.
A child lay clothed in a manger gown -
In David's city a heavenly boy.

A flight of cherubim came caroling.
Then in the nimbus sky relapsed conventional night.
Kind seraphim watched o'er the slumbering flock
While the shepherds visited a royal sight.

Nocturne

A rocky ledge
      Wolves on the edge
            Shepherds watch over lambs.

A quiet night
      An angel light
            Glory in the land.

A manger child
      Isaiah wild
            God with us.

The Noncollaboration

We could have lifted each other out of penury,
But you approached me as a dominance dilemma,
Whereas I was naught but love and charity.

November Tryst

When I all alone in melancholy sit
By the embers of a dying fire disconsolate,
I ponder how wealth and power hold kingly sway
And gain their ends through mindful favors pay
So I fear to venture out unwarmly wrapped
Lest on webs of influence I be trapped.
I look for a spark of friendship's loyal flame,
Discovered when I to your fireside came.
There you generous stoked the warming blaze
And did your friends with bounteous spread amaze.
Then merry banter round the hearth did fly
Till love to love ope'd windows in each eye.
So I your warm and faithful love remember
And banish thoughts of dolorous November.

"Now as a ghost of quaint-remembered time"

Now as a ghost of quaint-remembered time
I see you yet as it were yesteryear
When we gathered round in harvest medley chats
And exchanged fair friendship's bounteous cup of cheer.
Then you did part from out our hallowed grove
And ventured forth upon a stormy night.
I thought the place you left were ne'er repaired,
That all my aftering would dreary blight.
But now love dreams on in other minds.
It shapes my heart in bracing dayspring time.
Where once there were but few to treasure love,
Now are many found in heaven's rhyme.
Kindness kindles where sings the immortal choir
And hearts unite in faithful, babbling gyre.

Observations

An old man dozed in the waiting room
Of an interurban train station,
Cruising off his seat.

Two young lovebirds sat nearby,
The girl cooing -
The future rushing upon us.

A graduate of the Academy fiddled with the universe,
No, just scanned an opinion column,
Committing the ideas therein to memory.

Then a gaggle of prostitutes armed with fake love
Carried off all the little Pinocchios
It could discover.

October Thoughts

Rain falling
      Under the eaves
            I in my attic ruminate
                  Over dripping rainbow leaves.

Not enough love
      Melancholy drips
            Camping under the tarpaulin
                  Long ago on hunting trips.

Love is as love does
      The heavens are crying
            Plippety-plop steady gray
                  Tapping on the shadows sighing.

Then you come to clasp my hand,
And I transport to another land.

"Oft when I lay aside my scholar's books"

Oft when I lay aside my scholar's books
And dally in the halls of memory,
I reminisce upon our chance encounter
At a graduate student wine and cheese reception.
In conversational by-ways we laurel plucked
And set in wreaths upon each other's brow.
Then all around were wrapped in ecstasy.
Enchantment sat in chairs around the room
As we strolled about to retain the mystic moment.
When the clock struck ten, we bade each other goodbye
And retreated to our normal bookish lives.
The vision continued of your loving looks;
Shy certainty informed my reverie
On an exchange of vows and prayers for progeny.

Oxford Spires

Sunday chapel in academic gown
  A long sermon morosely read.

We are happy to go to brunch
  And socialize over the lacings of our lives.

In the afternoon the library opens its doors –
  Meditation in a medieval corner.

On the Passing of Village Elders

Oft in the course of gentle-pressing time
Social lions do suddenly pass away.
The step that boldly trod upon our rhyme
And voice in some dimension lacking sway –
These feared phenomena were canceled square.
I untouched still stand, in truth amazed.
With seeming heart and warming fair
They had looked on honor and noble blazed.
They had fought on in the age-old fight
Though in some dim-felt place unwise.
Deliver me from this same blight
That troubles men who strive for worldly prize.
You are the compassionate, unfathomed One.
You are my love and everlasting sun.

Past Glories

Old memories sleep in lilac letters.
    When I open one,
Out of a wispy scrawl
    Jumps a recognition.

The Patron Saint of Astronomers

The valley lay veiled in the mystic realms of night.
Dominic prayed, grappling with a dilemma.
Wakeful stars blinked in nonreply
While the landscape slept beneath a quiet sky.

Suddenly a luminous sphere effervesced above
And travelled earthward in its trajectory.
It came to rest over the abandoned hulk of a church,
St. Mary of Prouille, devoid of mystery.

Dominic wondered if this were an answer to prayer
And kept vigil a second and a third night.
When the light hovered again over the church,
He established a house for religious at the site.

The church restored, the Faith again awoke
When sisters befriended there the neighbor folk.

Patterns

A life traced in splendrous stars
Its course foretold by these silent philosophers …

An autumn leaf in perfection endowed
Its design enhanced by brilliant hues …

A footprint in the snow
A boot outlined to a marvel …

A checkered sky rippling with clouds
Whose blue dims the sapphire's excellence …

A sandy shore dotted with umbrellas
Whispering gaily to the billowing waves …

But when my life has traveled its course
In those seasons of repeated wonder,
The grandest design of all shall confront me,
The vision of the infinity of God.

(12/4/1960)

Peaches

A blossom floats on invisible eddies earthward
And then another.
Soon their fellows queuing for dismissal
Waft free to the ground.

Some time later spheres append
As if to try again –
Green, round, harvesting to russet gold.
These, however, fall a bit more abruptly.

Peregrinations

Light and Love ensconced in glory attire
Had pity on the feckless human race
Enmeshed in webs of power and tangled ire.
They bridged the great abyss on Christmas Day
And appeared in a world that had lost its Eden fire.

Vigilant pastors left their silly flocks
To angels incandescing in the sky.
Wise men left their ethnos and their land
To follow after heaven's starry trace
And hurry to the hidden glory place.

A Peripatetic Prayer

On a gray November afternoon
I happened on my mother at her peripatetic prayers.
She was walking crisply about the house
Saying the rosary out loud
And invited me to join the crowd.

And so we progressed past the Flower Madonna,
The Holy Family,
And Jesus leading children along a country path,
In single file from room to room,
Until at last we chased away the gloom.

Persephone

Soul shrieks wrenched to Hades.
      After many tears
            Grace cultivates the land.

"Petal grails decant a morning wine"

Petal grails decant a morning wine.
      Crystal drops disappear in the summer air.
         A bee arrives on dusty legs.

The Philharmonic

If all we knew were tympany,
From where would come that sound
That harmony devises
To mount a cantabile round?

If every man's an instrument
That plays on Nature's note,
Then you and I will find together
The chords that heaven wrote.

The Philodemic Society

When in the loom of faint-remembered time
I narrow gauge upon a distant track,
We meet again in sunny, smiling rhyme
And in that paneled chamber figure back.

You challenge now with bright and practiced eye,
Aim an argument to save the day,
Unlock a serried logic tilting high
And the rabble rouse into a hearty sway.

We fight on for the blue and gray,
Debating sharp the crux of bread and war,
You the Demosthenes of latter day,
I the keeper of a ratchet score.

Now as I listen to alma mater's bell,
I bless the time that friending you did spell.

The Piazza San Marco

A bevy of nuns flits across the square
While I sip a languid lemonade.
Souls dance in concentric circles.

On Pilgrimage

When I first met Sister Marian,
       She was celebrating fifty years.
              She had graduated from teaching history
                    To shepherding pilgrim dears.

She was a wee bit of a thing,
       But she knew of loving ways.
              She chattered on most amiably
                    To bless our Mayflower days.

The Pilgrim and the Troll

In an autumn cave
I discovered a troll.
          How droll!

He winked at me
And fell to anecdote.
          I laughed a whisper float.

We bantered light
Before a sparkle fire.
          Evanesced my desire.

I wanted nothing,
My self forgot
          And all such other fascined rot.

The Plot

The sinisters met to discuss the regression of man
To the level of a primal sensate.

"First we must deprive him of vocabulary,"
The sinisters webbed in cold and drear debate.
"We will erase the networks of his brain,
His Latin graces and Greek memory."

In the ensuing whirl of appropriate prevarication
They reduced man to a thatched villagery
Where he lived in congenial monosyllable.
Man groped toward clearings in the membrane.

"We will leave him in this state a while,"
The sinisters croaked around the drain,
"And, when he ceases so to hunt,
Attempt his further reduction to a grunt."

The Poem Child

A poem child
Slips a smile to me
To see if I comprehend.

It follies
By a mirror pond
To catch a dream or two

And laughs away
The jungle wild
With its flower sound.

A Poetry Reading

Les sanglots longs
Des violins
    De l'automne
Blessent mon coeur
D'une longueur
    Monotone.

You play fire
On the lyre
    Of my heart.

Tout suffocant
Et blême, quand
    Sonne l'heure,
Je me souviens
Des jours anciens
    Et je pleure.

You rehearse
A verse
    Eterne.

Et je m'en vais
Au vent mauvais
    Qui m'emporte
Deçà, delà
Pareil à la
    Feuille morte.

The rhyme charms,
The sense alarms,
    And I am mesmerized.

Pons Asinorum

For one man a Euclidean proposition,
For another the delicacies of the stomach.

The Portrait

My mother once saw the Holy Host
      In an aureole of light.
Thereafter she was everywhere on the lookout
      For this rare and delightful sight

In Paris she discovered a painting
      Of a roll of bread and glass of wine
Wherein a faint light shaped as a cross
      On the posterior wall did shine.*

This painting from the artist
      She hastened to acquire
And brought it home for family and friends
      To honor and admire.

*"Le pain et le vin"

The Presence

When in the grip of sad reality
I watch respect its gainful dicing play,
Then your presence inspires me to pray
And throw my soul into bright Divinity.

Your honey fount erases all despair,
And chary thoughts away will dissipate.
My aim is set beyond the constellate
As in the holy mysteries I share.

I wonder at your yearning for the Passion.
The answer comes, to eliminate the haze
That earthlings bring to the eternal gaze,
And let Love become once again the fashion.

Through your fount blithe heaven makes descend.
I whisper sweet nothings and on my knees do bend.

Quintin Castle

A craggy fortress showed its face
        to an angry Irish Sea,
And the sea swept close
        but not too close
Because the castle stood on rock
        and its base could ne'er be shattered.

With me it friendly shared
        its round of hospitality,
And I knew it ne'er would give o'er
        its crest, its shield nor its valiant name.

The Raconteur

Sir William, a superb anecdotalist,
Repaired our lacks
And shored up the dike of civilization
With his comical tacks.

He spoke the language of love.

The Radiance

A radiance looked out the ramparts of heaven
And created a race of men who were free,
But they did not understand how to love
And blundered into catastrophe.

The radiance dreamt
It could explain to men what it meant,
And so it visibled in human raiment.

151

Ramón y Cajal

He approached the nervous system painterly.
Goya, Velásquez, Murillo and El Greco
Would have understood.

Working with silver nitrate and gold sublimate,
He traced the finger of God
In his laboratory at home.

He cared nothing for cushioning his nest.
Peter of Alcántara, John of the Cross and Teresa of Ávila
Would have approved the investment.

He laid the histological foundations
Of modern neurology,
And for that they awarded him a Nobel Prize.

He had not always been so excited in the laboratory.
He had wanted to be a painter
And had been apprenticed to a barber.
Even in his medical studies he had proven
An indifferent scholar.

It was only later that the painterliness of it all
Fired his imagination,
And he began to visit the ateliers of heaven
Where the art displayed under his microscope
Awaited patient discovery.

At Random

I folded all my books,
Conversed the time away.
I canceled all my hopes
And set myself to pray.

God spoke at sundry intervals
To check my wayward drift.
I thought ahead to peak sublime
To close in us the rift.

Raymond of Peñafort

King James of Aragon took his mistress to Mallorca
Where he romped with his sybaritic court.
Saint Raymond remonstrated with the king
Against the scandal of his lustful sport.

The king declined to heed Saint Raymond's advice
So the friar decided to quit the royal satyr.
The king forbade sailors to assist him
And thought that was the end of the matter.

Raymond went to the shore and queried God,
Then flung defiance at the reach of power.
He attached his cloak to his staff and knelt thereon
And sailed away at thirty miles per hour.

His improvised craft bore him to Barcelona,
As witnessed on the shore by astounded folk.
Aragon heard the news and was impressed
And summarily dismissed his mistress much provoked.

On Reading Latin Authors

As autumn blows a brisker wind
And charms the leaves to rust and gold,
Pumpkins glow with candlelight,
And children play in the afternoon cold,
I retire to my country home
And there discover many a Latin tome.

"Otium sine litteris mors est."

I settle down amid books and papers
And visit with philosophers renowned
Who were of civilization the shapers.

"Philosophia est ars vitae."

I read the classics energetically
While you descend to an urban forum
To debate the issues in friendly rivalry.

"Dum in magna urbe declamas, mi amice,
scriptorem Troiani belli in otio relego."

I glean a harvest from these o'erlooked books
That harbor secrets in their paneled retreat,
A wisdom that belies their dusty looks.

"Debemus iram vitare."

In frivolous youth I spurned these friends,
Unaware of their magnificence.
Now I rue the day that here no time expends.

"Nihil sine magno labore vita mortalibus dat."

A scholar without pretentions,
I entertain in my hideaway
The poet pride of Rome and its extensions.

"Ratio me ducet, non fortuna."

Autumn's splendor is on the rampage
As I immerse in colloquies
With Cicero and the Sabine sage.

"Non solum eventus hoc docet
(iste est magister stultorum)
Sed etiam ratio."

Now winter's breath is in the air.
The trees have lost their lustrous veil.
I delve into treasure in my lair.

"Arma virumque cano."

Renaissance

We wake to fresh-beribboned break of day
Whereon the Creator has Aurora drawn.
Thrush and sparrow choir their amaze
As we linger bemused by rosy-fingered dawn.
The Designer awakens us to admiring awe
When silent mists of dewdrop shower
Bestow their touching tears on flower dress
And whisper kisses in a rosy bower.
Now the universe aglow with light
Persuades the past to unravel and erase
And lets the love that shines in heaven's eyes
Commune with the soul in an inner mystic space.
He knew our journey's ending long before
And all our sad regrets does kind unscore.

A Renaissance Man

Nicholas Steno had an affinity for the truth
And thus detected the secrets of anatomy.

Then Beauty bade him research geology
Where his science shattered hoary myth.

Through sunny Medici palaces he strolled,
Ruminating on the visions he had trolled.

He accessed the arches of Divinity
And plunged to the depths of the mysterious Trinity.

They exiled him a Quixote to wintry climes
Where on ascetic morns he woke to psalmody rhymes.

The Retreatmaster

In the soft crunch of freshly minted snow
A horse and buggy waited for a train
But they left as a fierce wind did blow.
Eventually Father Wojtyla did detrain
In the wee hours in a countryside icy cold.
As he hiked the road to his destination,
The darkness assaulted him with crystals bold.
His heart resorted to artillery
With a strong beat that pumped hot blood
Through channels into a capillary flood.
At length he circled a monastery tower,
Banging on doors for half an eternal hour.
Then the portress with a warm toss of light
Rescued him from the eerie claws of night.

The Reunion

All the old masters are gone,
Swept away like autumn leaves before the wind.

We attend a reception in the old abbey
Where everything has been subtly altered.

Half a century ago our mentors walked among us;
Now they have flown away into the sky.

We grasp at the ironies of time,
The tradition shrouded in memory.

The autumn leaves outside mock us
As we mix cocktails and conversation, past and present.

The darkness gathers around us so we cannot see
Shards of marigold and cerise separate from their boughs.

The stars are lit like bonfires in a far-away sky
As you, our docents, beam kindly thoughts to earth.

Reverie on Music

A dream floated on the verge
Of the sleeper's consciousness.
For a moment withheld,
It then spilled over the brink
To flood the imagination.

A piano's solitary note
Troubled the fog swamping his mind.
Slowly swirling,
Last fragments of twilight dispersed
As misty light centered upon two indistinct forms.

The pianist pressed a few random chords,
Preluding the first haunting tones,
While his admirer composed her rapt silhouette to listen.
Lightly she touched the instrument's ebony,
Absorbed in the recurring melody.

Now an eloquent stream gushed from his fingertips;
Frenzied thunder pealed from vibrant keys.
Intuitively the girl divined his every mood
And fantastic passion.
The sleeper, too, thrilled to the wild reverberations.

Again the performer altered his mood.
A compelling theme
Plunged into the calm pools of inmost thought.
The listener felt
Moonlight filter from an open casement.

The sonata's last passage
Drifted across the fanciful gloom.
The musical reverie
Dissolved among the gathering shadows,
And the dreamer relapsed into somber oblivion.

(6/5/1961)

Romance in the Black Forest

When in a pause in social conversation
I travel back to pastimes of our youth,
I recall the time when first our eyes caroused
To the gambol of a viol's happy strewth.
I wandered then from out the wall of friends
And met you on the promenade in flower.
We visited the baths of Roman days
And observed the valley from an antique tower.
We leisured o'er the choice of satin shoon,
Bought crystal fancies and brilliants in the mart.
You launched a chat o'er silver coffee spoon
And laughing watched my wade through whipcream tart.
We imagined when the emperor spoke in Latin
And society walked togaed on the matin.

The Round Tower

In an Irish vale the sky floats quiet by
While monks learn analects to apple-faced lads.
Diaphanous falls the cadence of an hour,
And Truth and Beauty joust around the tower.

Sudden-shock the bell sounds the fright.
They gather treasure and fly to the round tower.
It is the Dane. They sky-step out of rue
To elude his plunder and wild cry pursue.

They scale a ladder to a story above the ground.
The ladder inside, they lose themselves in prayer.
The Viking wanders the village of the wise
With nothing to pillage and none to terrorize.

Ryedale

When around the fire laughs a bon vivant
And jocund wags a tale ne'er false nor true,
I long to stir love's embers from their rest
And listen faint to heaven's voice in you.

The Sadist

When he traveled out of history,
He left a planet full of misery
And many a rotten memory.

And oh the glory of the Resistance!

My Sainted Mother

A transcendence floated past flower bowers
In Rocky River Park
And taught little dears in daylight hours
How to interpret many a mystery.
Twilights she floated on clouds of grace
In churches legacied by history.

Three quarters of a century later
Jeanne yearned for eternity.
Cancer – so decided to step off the planet my mater.
Her life transmuted into a sermon.
Lofted by prayer, she lapsed into smiles and laughter
And even some childhood German.

Then in a private moment with God
She floated off this mortal sod.

Saint Lucy's Day

When Scandinavians meet to fête with candles
On a cold December evening Saint Lucy's Day,
They laugh and sing and merrily converse
And chase the gloom of wintry days away.

Then sainted Ansgar, Olaf and Nicholas Steno
Beam down on their happy protégés
And channel blessings to and fro
To direct toward heaven their gaze.

Saint Martin's Summer

On an autumn lake
      Floats a drake
            Dreaming of a southern atoll.

Swallows fly by
      To a distant spy
            On a hemisphere stroll.

A friend laughs soft
      In my library loft –
            You are droll.

Saint Merry

When Burgundy was dark and wild,
I chose the life of prayer.
I learned a trade and letters too
And friended everywhere.

I taught the serfs the land to till,
To harvest milk and honey.
At country fairs they sold their wares
And made a lot of money.

The gentry lads came to our school.
I taught them ancient lore,
How heroes in the olden days
Did roam the Aegean shore.

When pilgrims came on patient feet
To say a hearty prayer,
I laughed and joked with all these folk
And merry tales did share.

I gloried in our chapel song
And before the host did bend.
Then in the twilight after hour
I laughed happily with a friend.

Once I went an anchorite
Into the forest deep,
And prayed alone to God by night
And dreamt an angel sleep.

To Paris did I elder go,
Again became the leaven,
Until at length with friends around
I homeward went to heaven.

Saint Valentine

When he was young and frolicked merry
Round tumbledown hills with other lads,
Love hedged him in a craggy redoubt
Where saints and heroes walked about.

He startled upward manly free
And gave himself to hearty charity,
Thereafter cared for orphan childs,
Loosed their shoon from tiger wilds.

At length the emperor caught him square,
Required a bow to stony gods.
He nothing thought but lofted high
And traveled homeward on a sigh.

Then Eden's rhythm did rebound
And Love no longer slunk around.

Saint Virgil

From Ireland did Virgil come
Unto the Frankish court,
Then wandered on to Salzburg
To challenge every tort.

Now Virgil knew geometry
And could measure earthly ends.
He verified the Grecian lore
That yon horizon bends.

He told the world that it was round,
But the world could not convince.
It forgave him since he meant so well
And named him bishop-prince.

So speak the truth but speak it soft
If you would win a life aloft.

Salzburg

Long ago I was intrigued by languages
And traveled to Salzburg for courses summery,
But it was the endeavors of leisure there
That now throng my memory.

At the Hohensalzburg fortress beneath the stars
Folk dancers drew us into their charmed mêlée.
Afterwards we chatted over their travels
At a lanterned outdoor pub soirée.

I went to a Mozart Mass on a Sunday
Where angels and archangels sang in choirs,
Assisting mere human voices in the rendition.
Heaven floated in Salzburg's spires.

On a hike we decided to ascend a mountain peak.
A man in lederhosen ran up the mountain
And on his downward dash stopped to say
That he climbed at this pace almost every day.

I acquired a dirndl with a rosy apron.
And wore it around the music festival town
Where there were other dirndls on the street
And in the evenings many a fashionable gown.

One afternoon we attended "Everyman,"
Performed with the cathedral as a backdrop.
We followed this time warp into the Middle Ages
And discovered ourselves in the plot.

I encountered in the street some hometown friends
Who had come to Austria to collect their son.
We pondered the cuisine at an outdoor café
And discussed their impending Italian vacation.

We visited the archbishop's hunting lodge
Where a youthful Mozart made his concert rounds.
We discovered the archbishop's quaint sense of humor
As we walked about the English garden grounds.

I thought Austria was a corner of heaven
And on the earth might be a happy leaven.

Scholar Days

Students emerge from the surrounding town,
      Walk through a gate into a gowned renown.

They attend a lecture and take hasty notes
      And chat with friends as they shift their totes.

They consult hidden library lore,
      Papers last rifled decades before,

And delve into matters suitably recond,
      Surfacing hourly for a human bond.

The bell rings, and they walk through the din
      Into another exciting imagine.

The Scholar Knight

When the zest for tournament descends to plod,
Many a scholar travels on a dare
Out his turret with a view of heaven
Into the tormented public square.

His questing desert sword unmanly lowered,
He ventures forth to play with heritage.
Late his face has crumpled to a frown
Till he clambers back to his faithful hermitage.

There he wonders on the stars at night,
Muses on a glorious eternity.
He walks the paths of love with kindred souls
And joys to trust in kind Divinity.

He had dallied with an earthly gleam,
Had delayed the tryst with everlasting dream.

The Schoolmistress

And the one who bent her will to love,
Though none on earth should know,
With the first among the saints above
Shall ring on harp touch slow.

The Seaport

One afternoon we visited the wharf
To gaze upon a Viking's olden sail.
We learned about a stormy ocean crossing,
How in the wind there quaked a giant flail.

You led me then through dockside merchantry
With articles from out the world's display
We admired antiques and their replicas
And chatted half the afternoon away.

The love that then your voice full subtle spoke
Does now this memory full glad evoke.

The Secret of Happiness

A thorn stabbed at my soul.
The rain was charged with pain.
Circled round a troll.

When I offered up the pain,
A heavenly Hand swooped low
To lift away the chain.

So vanished troll and thorn
And rainbows hung around.
It was a joyful morn.

Serendipity

I never had a wealth of friends.
I never had a golden heraldry.
Yet one day I chose to love
And happened on the mystery.

169

The Shamrock Lady

I met a loving Irish lass
Who had a loving heart,
And everything she did for me
Was loving from the start.

She wined and dined me at her hearth
And served a sauce of talk.
I'll ne'er forget her happy laugh
Nor blarney on a walk.

She shared with me her Irish lore,
Drew castles in the sky,
And when I cared to live in them,
She winked a merry eye.

The Shepherd Boy

The lambs browse by
         The wolves beware
                  I watch upon a hill.

A whisper nigh
         A chuckle rare
                  The inky night lies still.

The heavens resplend
         Glories bend
                  To praise a manger babe.

The Shepherd Lad

Night descends.
> An angel bends.
>> I go.

A maiden with a lantern light
> Contemplates her tender wight.
>> God works a miracle.

We pastors kneel
> For the joy we feel.
>> God directs.

The innkeeper stays awake
> To tabulate his take.
>> God observes.

Burghers drowse on woolen blankets toss,
> Staunch avoid the cross.
>> God is silent.

Morning unveils,
> Cloaks starry pales.
>> I depart.

The world is on a changing track,
> And wolves press forward to attack.
>> I know eternity awaits.

The Siege of Belgrade, 1456

When cannon daggers crashed through craggy walls,
And blades of janissaries flashed their spite,
And Muslim shouts impressed the populace,
Still John Capistrano held high the invisible light.

They fingered holds in the aged, crumbling stone.
Searched out apertures through which to plunge.
They sought to extinguish the iridescent flame,
The laugh, the joke, with one rapacious lunge.

John was too high; the sky they could not reach.
They lacked a ladder to attempt the celestial scale.
The old man taught his men to walk with God.
The light encircled yet the Holy Grail.

As the adversary surged through the outer walls,
And frightened townsfolk to river boats repaired,
The defenders launched downhill a fret of fire.
In a bramble hell the Sultan's men despaired.

When John stood firm, his men evinced their might
And repelled the foe with a stalwart inner light.

"Since first you broached you would a voyage make"

Since first you broached you would a voyage make
And shared the news you had a chasm crossed,
The chestnut, all its highstrung beauty lost,
Has scattered tatters on an autumn lake.

The day breaks drear when we must say farewell.
With rapid speech I spend my love's relate.
My heart has withered now to serried state
And steads itself to meet the stern compel.

The clouds do tumble when we forcèd part.
The air lies still in muffled, bated breath
To note the tragedy of friendship's death,
The ungracious cooling of a wayward heart.

I raise my eyes unto the tearing skies
And think eternal thoughts with less surprise.

The Sky Dweller

Twenty stories high,
I glance across to other castles in the sky
Whose drawbridges are manned by jacket and tie.

Who is the chatelaine of yonder suite?
Perhaps I will encounter her by the moat one day
Or at a society soirée.

One day our eyes meet, and I friendly feel.
She turns away and draws the tapestry.
Perhaps I am not of her tribe and family tree.

Sky Pillows

Whipcream yachts sail in an airy sea,
       Wooly lambs wander toward the dawn,
             Cottonball billows stage a sunset show.

Scenery changes
       While we are anchored
             By thrifty gravity.

Snares

Anthropos was wandering in an obscure wood
When suddenly he observed the Theos light
In a distant clearing.

He tried to reach the brilliance,
But the way led through the Logos,
And honey-laden intercepts
Clung to his accoutrements.

Until he thrust beyond his comfort zone,
He glimpsed the light at best elliptically.

The Snow Maiden

A lady walked in an oak tree grove,
Paused watchful on a knoll,
While flakes of snow drifted down
To grace her winter stroll.

She cradled in her mantle warm
A child divine and frail.
She vanished in a luminesce –
I beheld the Holy Grail.

The Song of Demeter

In love's recess,
     Interruption, mourning,
          Grey gloom on sky-blown scape
               Dead, all is dread.

When love returns,
     Free flowing tresses
          Blossomy with pinks
               Alive, all shall thrive.

A Southern Belle

In melancholy rain she plucked magnolias
Huddled against the importune.
She whimsied love as blossoms
Drenched in tears.

Time unclocked, leisure attendant,
Her face, the chronicle of delectation,
Slipped into smiles.

Spaces

In the olive groves of Bethlehem
There walked a maiden child,
Creating spaces where Love might dwell
By fasting, prayer and mercy mild.

She chatted in the marketplace –
A subtle maiden child –
Creating spaces where men might live
Outside the trace of jungle wild.

She managed with scant hostelry –
A kindly mother child –
Creating spaces where God might live –
A boy from heavenly joys exiled.

The Starfisher

She wept among the moonbeams
And, garbed in dulcet tone,
Broke touch with those who prey.

She waded in among the stars
To grasp at shards of light,
And left no trace on the dusty shore.

The Stoic

To lose the reassurance of property,
The recompense of a gainful life,
I cannot without tears.
When virtue weakens, affability dies.
Then violence stabs at convention,
The thousand irrelevancies ring redundant,
The pith of argument circles on itself,
Bloody pretense paints elliptic misconstrue,
And deadly chaos orbits the planet.
A Stoic dagger may yet wing me clear.
The test o'er, score totaled, freedom cancelled,
Man doffs this raiment of dust,
This identifying disguise lent by Nature
That hung so freshly in youth
But dilapidated with age.
The essential man, unmasked in the end,
Views the ancient verities.
The deadly blade keys a door I cannot close again.
O bless my soul! What hellish smirk greets me there?
Is it the devil? Have I journeyed so far
That I already roast in Hades?
A lamp, a light, assistance here.
I will round about and see where lies the exit.
This gloom lacks space enough and egress.
I must climb a bit or swill in the muck,
O'erweighed in the dross of years,
When artifice of downside friends
Helped me to a fall.

Strayed sapients

Strayed sapients brave the Stygian cross.
They fend off the call of Love
And ferry on to eternity.

Stuhlweissenburg, 1601

Laurence of Brindisi was the chaplain general
Of the Christian troops defending Hungary.
They were beleaguered by Mohammed's host
And in the throes of penultimate despair.

Heavily outnumbered and ensconced in battlements,
The troops watched Laurence ride up and down the front
Armed with a crucifix and a prayer.
He braved death like a stag before the hunt.

Enemy cannon roared and muskets cracked.
Around Laurence their shots fell to the ground.
Arrows sped toward his trusting heart,
But dropped to earth without their target found.

The Christian defenders sought his proximity,
There where angels fought and safety lay,
Where bullets dropped in their trajectory.
They thought to keep voracious death at bay.

After five days of probing the saint's defenses,
Mohammed tired of the logic of his sword.
He bowed to fate and withdrew from Hungary
While Laurence retired to praise and thank the Lord.

The Sun

The sun moves in measured orbit across the sky
Or is it we who roll about the universe
Angled oddly round our planet
Whirling at uncanny speed
To meet and pass him every day
Even wobbling a bit to ensure asymmetry.

And so we stand unsteadily on solid ground
That moves in three calculus directions.
How disoriented we become to think
That the sun moves also.

The Surprise Wedding

A lily found in a craggy bound
Laments her sad predicament.

She desires to marry yet none will tarry.
She eyes the default - life on a shelf.

Screams an owl imps on the prowl.
She elects honor deselects the grim.

A proposal floats and the lady consents.
The Creator invades the maid
Who married lives happily ever after.

"Swift on an angel rhyme"

Swift on an angel rhyme
In quaint December
With its frosty lace
And snowflake quilt,
A cave sits warm with bated breath
While the unimagined throw
Shatters teardrop time.

Sympathy

Stormy seasons in a December land
Left me feeling dreary and less grand
Until you transcended into my concerns
And lent a friendly helping hand.

Symphonia Vitae

The Divine Hand
Which composed the great symphony
Of human life
And presently conducts it
Will one day signal the last chord
To consummate its themes and discords.

It directs a masterpiece
Of various movements
Representing the centuries of men
And moods
Signifying the darkling evolution of thought
And philosophical patter
Which provides the central theme
Motivating all harmony and dissonance.

The Divine Eye
Views the various instruments
Of men's idle minds
And the chorus of men's paltry opinions
Surveys the score
Assures that the softest flute
Contributes its note
To the orchestra's endeavor.

These strike forth vigorously
Then fade away
Replaced by other prevailing melodies.

The Divine Conductor
Does not remain coldly aloof
But, exacting in His direction,
Controls the errant fantasies
Of His unruly orchestra,
Lacing it into an effective whole.

Following the completion of the symphony
An eternity will be spent
Listening to its echoes.
Its harsh dissonances
Will clash on the ears of hell,
Its triumphal reverberations
Swell out over the celestial realm –
The amphitheatre of God.

(12/4/1960)

Television in the Olden Days

Saint Kenneth befriended many a saint
In Ireland, Wales, Scotland and Rome.
These were the men with whom he studied
And with whom he felt at home.

One day his friend Saint Columba
Went sailing with his confreres.
A storm began to toss their ship
So everyone set to his prayers.

Far away in Ireland,
Kenneth leapt up from his dinner.
One shoe fell by the way
As he ran to the church to pray.

Columba told his confreres what had happened
And that God would listen to Kenneth
Who trusted in his apprehend
As he rushed to save his saintly friend.

Tenebrae

As the lights relinquish one by one their hope
To the twilight's sad surround,
And the wakeful night makes pensive
The reminisce of day,
Let us light our tapers, friend,
From the bright and darting flame of love
Until the Dayspring childs in wild morningtide.

Thanksgiving

On Thanksgiving Day they gathered around
And asked the Lord for a blessing,
Then passed the turkey in a mound
And everyone had some dressing.

The hostess spoke a joke so merry,
The company fell to laughing.
She poured again a Spanish sherry,
And everyone did some quaffing.

The folk exchanged her joke for joke
Until the candles fell.
Then they thanked her every bloke
And wished her ever so well.

Thérèse of Lisieux

The Little Flower was Jeanne's favorite saint.
Thérèse was hardy, fun and caring.
She wrote an autobiography.

She made of her life a "little way" to heaven,
Not a fireworks in history
As Joan of Arc had lived it.

And so Jeanne took the name Thérèse
Upon her confirmation.

Thoughts on Immortality

When in the twilight of a blustery afternoon
I think winter thoughts of grave philosophy,
Then laughter echoes in the memory
And contradicts the pains of gravity.

I troll vast tomes for proofs and evidence
And elude the traps of convincing counterrhyme.
Love hovers expectant on the rim of the world
As I question the power of rapscallion Time.

At length I espy faint traces of the Eternal
And can trust the reports of immortality.
Love will cancel the grotesqueries of death
When I step off the planet out of history.

Traces

The greatest pleasure,
> The greatest gain,
>> Is to follow the trail of stardust
>>> Down an obscure country lane.

A Tragedy of Improvisation
Saint Raymond of Peñafort (1175-1275)

Raymond was Master General and a lawyer
When one day he decided to improvise,
To resign as the head of the Dominicans
And quiet contemplation prioritize.

He had his counselors agree to a rule
That resignation for cause must be accepted.
The following year he resigned, citing age.
The counselors felt they could not reject it.

Raymond retired to his home priory
And there busily worked for thirty-five years
Until God finally let him off the planet.
He had painstakingly paid his arrears.

Transcendence

Violet hues etched the threatening range
As the sunlight prepared to depart.
A cloudless sky glowered
During the sphere's plunging descent.
Stingingly the shadows touched my fingertips,
And the icy embrace of Himalayan blasts
Searched my coat to steal its warmth.
Yet long did I stay there at the peak,
Watching darkling cloaks settle on craggy rifts.
The shrill breath of these monstrous mountains
Shrieked in the ravines' ragged contours,
Jolted a newborn avalanche …
Thundered in the vengeful fury of Nature upon Man.

Yet I pondered aloof the wanderer,
Reviewed rude and primitive majesty,
Thrilled at its puissant solemnity,
Still unstirred by its attempt to shatter my soul …

At length retracing some solitary climber's steps
Upon the raw and luminous snow,
He strode in wonder, even now
Attending the voice of the isolated heights.
Deluded by the savage strain,
He left the ploughed furrows
And strayed unheeding into the enigma
Of somber oblivion.
Sudden clouds arose from the white ridges;
Their laden stillness unloosed a flurried storm,
After which human eyes
Ne'er again beheld the mystic stranger.

(1960)

Travels

It's a merry trip to England,
To where the angels are,
And many a flight had I taken,
Had it not been so far.

I traveled there imagining,
To Oxford and fair Cambridge too,
In many a dream have I set down
In London 'fore I knew.

A Turnover in Friends

When first we met, you were wearing a colorful blanket
Which announced your provenance from Africa.
I politely refrained from commenting on your garb,
And you helped me with a difficult French translation.

We kept in touch only at Christmastime
Until one day your excited letter arrived.
You needed confirmation of employment,
And I was able to help you on this side.

Thereafter we remained only Christmas friends.
Summers you came through on a working vacation.
You were dedicated to your inspiration
And did not leisure outside of your vocation.

I meant nothing to you, so I thought.
Friends are useful and then they are not.

The University Club

He had graduated half a century ago
And now was retired from the workaday world.

He opined on questions of the day
Before a pine log fire.

"I travel now on memory," he told me.

A man approached to shift the logs.
A burst of sparks flew up the chimney.

"The Chinese call those fire flowers," he commented.

His wife had passed away.
The children all had flown.

"Home is in the heart of a friend," he observed.

The Utopian

He walked the metaphysical network,
Ready to catch darts or deflect them.
He coaxed fire from heaven
To warm the heart of friends,
Putting love in at the silt end of things.

Dark brood collapsed self
Shakes itself and takes wing.

My Valentine

When in the winnowing of a windy winter's day
I walk alone through a throw of snow,
I feel inspired against the assault to pray
And turn within to the Benevolence I know.

You are my own dear one with a loving plan.
You rescue me from the fate of a cardboard man
Who lacks the blessing of interiority
And ventures forth in drear sobriety.

I laugh to think that blasting winter's grate
Mere serves to shift me to Your contemplate.

Valentine's Day

When on a dreary winter afternoon
We dwell o'er long on Nature's ragged dress,
Then Love comes to charm a nascent prayer,
And we remember the One Who cancels all distress.
The promise of joy checks the strain of rain
And makes us recognize in dross the gain.
So now we work to expand the circle of love
And in our midst detect blithe heaven's glove.

The Vanishment

Olive trees visibled at dawn.
An idle moon evanesced in the sky.
Guards vigilled for thievery
And nodded o'er their swords.
A still figure wrapped in a sheet
Lay on a sepulchre slab.

The earth quaked, the guards collapsed,
And light burst out the tomb.
The lifeless body warmed and stirred
And vanished from the shelf of history.
Out of their wits, the guards played dead.
The drama done, they random fled.

Then an angel rolled away the entrance stone
And with kind women held colloquy.

The Verger

He walked not high enough.
He stepped not proudly humbly through the fire.
He came not close enough to where
Inspiration laps at human shore.
He reached not far enough
Beyond the unsurprised
And found not through enough a line.
He raced not fast enough but lagged behind
Until the harpies caught him
And turned him into a cadaver
Twisting in the wind.

Veritas

Saint Dominic took Truth as his motto and his passion.
While contemporaries rejected their heritage,
He discovered the Truth and its kindly ends
And found this policy paid dividends.

A miracle worker and cheery raconteur,
He gravitated to universities.
He attracted the wise with tales of Divinity
And the faithful with works of lightning prodigy.

Food mysteriously appeared in a mountain pass.
He pentecostalized into German,
Rescued the dying and restored life to the dead.
Thus men came to believe what Dominic said.

Where the fire of love had careless, neglected died,
Dominic the forgotten flames revived.

The Vigil

Trolling the heavens for signs of astrology,
Wise men found the Eterne.
The universe knocked akimbo
Was nudged back into symmetry.

Vigiling

Shepherds watched on a lonely hill,
Their flock sequestered 'neath the stars.
They wakeful held the wolves at bay.
How still and silent Bethlehem lay!
Careless burghers snored in their beds.

Then all at once an angel flashed up the sky
And told of the Saviour that lay in manger hay.
A cherubim choir raised a glory shout.
The raptured shepherds hastened to obey,
Discovered the stable where Love held court that day.

Vigils

Watching for wolves,
Kind shepherds happened on a premiere.
Observing the starry complex,
Wise men chanced on Divinity reflects
Whilst other folks flipflopped in their beds.

The Village

They say all the great sorrows are dumb,
And so I somber seriatim gaze
At coffeehouses boasting foreign lapel
Where clockwise chats a theater clientele.

You and I stroll this cabaret town,
You remarking on Edna St. Vincent Millay
And where she lived; she lived everywhere,
On narrow streets with friends in close repair.

You tell me that writers frequent a certain tavern
And abstract a play to drowse away the even.
We find a table in the vicinity
And talk of letters and Greek antiquity.

I think when friendship cheery entertains,
My heart its voice and melody regains.

Vilnius

From Castle Hill I descry
Medieval streets
Winding through strata of history.

I visit the dreams of architects,
The crust of centuries,
The evidence of prosperity.

I reminisce the Grand Duchy
And its courtly resplend,
Retrace the confluence of East and West
And civility's ascend.

To a Violin

O violin! Memory of neglected love,
Cadences in cascade,
Chords of a heart
Abandoned and sobbing copiously.

O violin! Voice of our ancestors
Murmuring a forgotten theory,
A melodious inspiration
That makes the verities tremble.

O violin! Thought of a distant lover,
Joy upon sighting
A directing star

Among the abstractions of sound.

Visitations

Watchful shepherds
    Serenaded by angel choirs
        Walked on cushions of air

And wise men
    Lanterned by a star
        Trundled into history

While careless burghers
    Slumbered in their beds
        Drowning in weights of frown.

Visiting in the Village

Down in the crunch of a distant warp in time
We ferried thoughts from libraries of old
Like scholars trundling spindly notes abroad
From the crumble of aging parchment gold.

Through the television blinked a chitchat quiz.
You won the prize in every fresh foray.
Then silken voices sifted through opinion.
We clambered high in cultural mêlée.

So grew we close obeying friendship's law
While night crept close, its claw in silent awe.

Wanderers Nachtlied

Über allen Gipfeln
ist Ruh,
in allen Wipfeln
spürest du
kaum einen Hauch;
die Vögelein schweigen im Walde.
Warte nur, balde
Ruhest du auch.

Johann Wolfgang von Goethe

Wanderer's Night Song

The mountaintops
Are silent.
In the treetops
You feel
Hardly a breath.
Little birds are silent in the woods.
Only wait. Soon
You too will rest.

[A close translation]

Wanderer's Night Song

The mountaintops
Are cloaked in silence.
The treetops
Stir
With barely a breath.
The thrush is silent in the wood.
Only wait. Soon
You too shall rest.

[The emotion evoked by sound in German is evoked by vocabulary
in English.]

"When Aelred walked the valley of the Rye"

When Aelred walked the valley of the Rye
And discoursed fine on friendship and on love,
The margent rang with chants to reach the sky
And the moor was flush with sheep and gentle dove.
History marched beyond the valley rim
But troubled not the dwellers in that dale.
They worked the Creator's touch on earth to limn
While Eden peered round every haystack bale.
And if that yesterworld encompassed sorrow,
They translated it to access pools of grace
Until the jesting light of heaven's morrow
Should all unkind vicissitudes erase.
Now as autumn drifts across the silent vale,
We search the close for traces of the Grail.

"When a voyager in this heady place of dreams"

When a voyager in this heady place of dreams
Halts upon the margent of menacing death
And reflects upon a past that begs forget,
A conscience that sleeps in bogs of discontent,
Long winters of grave debauchery
That toyed with death like the sword of Damocles,
Then Divine Love breaks out on his exile
And bathes his face in a heavenly smile.

"When evening trips across the starry sky"

When evening trips across the starry sky,
I wonder on your daydreams by and by
And if your ship has sailed the seas apace,
Led by dreams to its destined place.

Have you juggled jagged gems of thought?
Have you caught the pearls that I have taught?
Rich fare and opulent merchantmen
Ply the waves for troves that fame the pen.

I hazard you crest a vocabulary sea
To defend a civilization's integrity.
You quest for love in troubled foreign waters
And thwart the shafts of Mnemosyne's wayward daughters.

I dream alone and pray that God will send
You inner lights that your fortunes mend.

"When first we met in labyrinthine night"

When first we met in labyrinthine night,
While distant orbs trained down on earth their rays,
In that felicitous and tranquil light
My eyes alit on your immortal ways.
Heaven directed our looks through ardent eyes
So that they found their sights without beguile.
Enchantment dropped from out the starry skies
And angels fluttered in a moonbeam aisle.
I fell entranced before your sovereign grail
And silent watched with the blessed night.
My grappled heart did sudden light grow frail.
I gazed on you astonished with delight.
When darkness sought to veil your brilliance,
Your light of love increased in radiance.

"When I all alone in somber sorrow sit"

When I all alone in somber sorrow sit
Before a fire in fading embers lit,
I grope about in faithless memory
For shards of humor to dispel the misery.
Long ago I fled conventional thought,
And now I am in trepidation caught.
Then I remember your champagne ebullience
On evenings spent in private audience.
You recalled a comic professorial moment
And imitated a classic scholars' foment.
I listened happily to your prattle
That armed me fresh for the daily battle.
The mem'ry of your love draws me higher
And makes me smile as I stoke the fire.

"When in the course of unrelenting time"

When in the course of unrelenting time
I travel through the vales of memory,
I betimes elude the brace of levity
And shed hot tears o'er past improbity.

Besieged by Eros, my skiff ran fast aground,
And farce came nipping at my slipping feet.

Then trips a thought into my vagrant mind
That renders life again sublime and sweet.

The sins of yesteryear were best forgot
For the fulsome mess has been oblivioned by our God.

"When in the fray of a wayward and chaotic time"

When in the fray of a wayward and chaotic time
I cross your threshold a melancholy sight,
I pray you remember my combat against the night
And listen the knell of the eternal chime.
In a fathom faint of lovely compline sound
And the shutting of a refulgent sunset eye,
Your heart attends a weary pilgrim's cry
And hastens to unlatch your castle ground.
I sometimes lack what legacies can endow,
The dash and flash of golden luxury,
But ne'er your offset of my penury
Nor the mystic rhyme that love and faith allow.
And should your thoughts devolve to swift repay,
Recall the joy of the mystic roundelay.

"When in the grip of a wild and darkling night"

When in the grip of a wild and darkling night
I reflect upon the vanishing ghost of time,
I think then on the cave of Bethlehem
And what happened there beyond the reach of grime
For there a child was born to bring us grace
And right the wrong that had long o'erta'en our race.

201

"When in the reminisce of a long-forgotten time"

When in the reminisce of a long-forgotten time
I happen on a sunny memory
And pleasure in the charm of bygone days,
I sashay away from emotional penury.

Recalling the joy of childhood holidays
I exorcise an imp and his gloomy.
Forgetting the bitterness of dreams awry,
I remember the promise of heaven's ecstasy.

A lade of bliss and one of uncertainty
Brings me to my present quandary.
Should I be sad or merry in this instance
Or choose to be merry no matter the circumstance?

The good man is happy, says Aristotle,
So I go forward in life with happiness as my model.

"When in the retrospect of a distant time"

When in the retrospect of a distant time,
I counterpoint upon a windowpane,
The puzzle of the present comes alive,
And I understand the ancestral emotional pain.

They passed their ire down the generations,
Were ignorant of the mystic roundelay
Where God and man mingle in a union
And levitate above the sodden gray.

"When in the vise of elder-drifting time"

When in the vise of elder-drifting time
Fortune hides her face and sometimes turns away,
I hasten to your warm and faithful hearth
Where friends speak love in melodious roundelay.

We air some theories of political economy,
You tell me of your favorite poetry,
We comment on the latest films from Cannes
And medieval provincial tapestry.

As I after dwell on friendship's kindly face
And heaven taste in your levity,
I think we have lofted high and ebullient
And set aside the law of gravity.

When we are gone and laid to earthly rest,
This verse remembered remembers me your guest.

"When in the winter of our experiment"

When in the winter of our experiment
We falter and begin to lose our way,
We remember the saints who passed before
And regain the path to the mystic roundelay.

"When summer faints upon an autumn trail"

When summer faints upon an autumn trail,
With sad surprise I reflect upon our tale.
Once we were young and merrily innocent.
We hunted berries till the day was spent.
But those sunny hours long away have sped.
Now we're caught in a net that checks our tread.
We are trapped in the warping skein of time
That prevents regress save in this faltering rhyme.
In improvisations that happened out of sight
You fled our childhood pastimes and delight.
I ken beneath the smiling mask a fiend
Where once an angel a loving harvest gleaned.
Could I but turn the clock to yesteryear
And ransom you with love and summer cheer!

"When the fruits to labor are denied"

When the fruits to labor are denied,
And autumn's harvest yields a slender sheaf,
Then melancholy thoughts the ploughman chide
And doubts dispel his primal spring belief.
I wondering slump 'gainst gnarlèd oak and moan,
Sad volumes ope' and page about my brain,
To think how slipped the sown onto a stone
And why in fecund soil sleeps the grain.
When reason and the whims of Fate collide,
I think it is to keep me humbly by.
To wrest a man secure from tumbling pride
The laurel must the enchanted crowd deny.
I reflect that in another century
We'll all have fled this hapless penury.

"When thoughts immortal descend to mortal strand"

When thoughts immortal descend to mortal strand
And dreams of glory o'erwhelm the earthly dross,
I forget the hazards of mad fortune's way,
And joys transluce what seemed a heavy cross.
Then the world of grappling chance and fitful rue
Snatches at my clothes to drag me down.
I adopt the antics of an Aristophanes,
The trappings of a melancholy clown,
To evoke a laugh from a once indifferent crowd,
To lift the spirits of the audience
And raise the siege of sorrow on the earth,
The gloomy legacy of decadence.
In this masquerade of sprightly comedy
I glimpse the bliss of bright eternity.

Wild Swans

A dirt road accessed a wilderness lake.
Experiments in domestic rusticity
Rose here and there along its shores.
When we appeared on a deck by the water's edge,
A family of swans paddled in our direction.

Our hostess gave us each some bread
To distribute to our feathered visitors.
It was a father and mother and two gray cygnets.
The cygnets floated between their parents.
Our hostess said there used to be six in the clutch.

The father snapped crumbs from our hostess' hand
And bolted down his take.
The mother gobbled up morsels landing in the water
Before her offspring could wolf them down.
The father deferred only to his mate in breakfasting.

The mother was in defense mode, her wings upraised,
The entire time they were in our sight.
Some feathers were missing from her panoply,
A sign that she had fought for her children
When the hawks came swooping down.

Later we saw the family paddle across the lake.
The father led in defense mode.
The two offspring followed one by one.
The mother brought up the rear,
Also in defense mode.

Instinct and power ruled in that family of swans
Entirely bereft of Christian charity's bonds.

A Winter Child

In poverty kept
> A child slept
>> A maiden wept for joy.

Kind angels glowed
> The nightfall snowed
>> A mother showed her boy.

A blessed trove
> A thorny cove
>> A love without alloy.

A Winter Field

A field lies barren on a winter day.
On the farther edge a ridge of forest
Interrupts the sky,
A distant gray turbulence
Aroused and desolate.

A field lies inanimate in the cold air,
Stern and speechless,
No insect colonies transferring pollen
And softening the soil,
No minutiae alive.

A field lies fallow waiting for spring,
Stalks broken and disorderly,
Impeccably dressed in tattered rags,
Having recourse to philosophy
While men converse by the hearth.

The Winter Plum Tree

Three sages wrapped them close
      By Old Wang's embering fire,
Sipped their cups of mellow wine
      To the graceful notes of a flute.
A tumble of snow lay soft
      Upon the mountain sea
While firelight flickered faces
      Amid the charms of a lute.

They dreamt of wild cranes
      Flying on a lotus wind.
            Warming flamed the hearth.

Old Chu thought a lady with her child
      Had mildly stirred without
And arose to find a winter plum tree
      Flowering in the snow.
He called his friends
      And they remarked
The blossoms' tremble light
      In flurried snowflake blow.

They dreamt of wild cranes
      Flying on a lotus wind.
            Warming flamed the hearth.

The three retired late
      From their bouts of conversation,
The wonder of winter plum flowers
      On every drifting thought.
Sweet sifted through their dreams
      That olden winter night
The winter flowers from heaven
      In fine imagine caught.

When I thought
    Of this crack in history,
        Warming flamed my heart.

The Winter Sea

Gray rolled the slowly surfing shore.
Rain dropped soft into the vast and waiting sea.
This was the end of quaint biography –
Driftwood washed up on the shoals of history.

A Winter Sprite

Down at the end of winter when the clear, cold rivulets run,
Beneath the snow's escarpments beside the Avalon,
Down there I sudden met an aged and hoary sprite
Who sat upon an icicle throne before a crystal sun.

"Grandfather," quoth I, "have you a word to the wise?"
"I have," saith he, "but many do it despise."
"How may I right the wrong that's crept into history
And cancel the debts that chain men to such misery?"

"Young sir," saith he with a fiery eye
Cast on that wintry scene,
"Prostrate before the Mighty One
And implore the Maiden Queen."

A Wintry Fantasy

The surly wind
Buffets the naked trees.
The wintry sun
Cold light casts on a colder scape.

Homes defended by tall evergreens
Present ancient walls
To the howling wind.
And inside the snug homes, smug people
Thank the Lord for green hope and the mind
When all else is a despairing waste.

Trees
Their limbs stenciled on
The iron sky –
Lacework finely stitched –
veins reaching, groping into nothing –
And a tangle
Of twisting, groaning boughs
Etched in shades of black
Against the wind
And the gloom
Unshattered by sunlight.

The dreary world's a place
Where no soul
May rest.
Trudging the barrens and blundering too often,
Weary souls will be gathered
To their fulfillment.

(1960)

A Win-Win Game

It's the happy way to heaven
That's surest and most true,
And as we stride along that way,
Let's company sans rue.

The scene that we are playing
Is of a noble cast.
To act with faith and hope and love
Brings happiness at the last.

And when we're all in heaven
And feel that blissful state,
We'll helpless love each other
In joyous contemplate.

There's no need to wait for heaven
To be friends beyond compare,
For all it takes is a loving heart
And hands that want to share.

So if we're happy for each other,
And love is all we know,
We'll joyous dance in heaven's streets
And gain the reap of sow.

A Wonder

Spring arrived this morning.
At sunset a promise floated in the air.
By daybreak the trees were flower-veiled.
The trees have become champagne
And I am high again.

The Woolies

They had had spaces creep in among them
Where woolies gathered of snarling gray.
In friends' surround there was no outward sign.

When the Huns came to pillage and destroy,
The young men joined the Resistance
While their sisters worked in the local hospital.

And one night, laughing around the fire,
They discovered all the woolies were gone
And there were no more sad spaces.

A Worldly Maneuver

Tolstoy's older brother noticed his vocation
And took him to a brothel.
He did not want his little brother
Ahead of him in matters spiritual.

And so Tolstoy acquired a weakness
He had not previously had.
He still had a penchant for the ascetic life
Plus now a length of sad.

The Worldly Young Governor of Perugia

Captured by the enemy,
John Capistrano stood in pools of water,
Chained to a dark and dank dungeon wall.

Shot through with pain from a fracture
Sustained during an escape attempt,
The worldly young governor of Perugia finally fainted.

He awoke to a dazzling aura of light
That framed a figure in Franciscan robes.
When the vision faded, he discovered his golden locks
Were cropped short in friar fashion.

No, no, no, no! he shouted inside.

A week passed.
His situation ameliorated.
He was allowed a doctor and better quarters.
Perhaps he would be ransomed.
Invisible fingers unraveled the stylish raiment
Of the worldly young governor of Perugia.

Then St. Francis returned.
This time he reproached John
For not acceding to his new calling.

Yes, yes, yes, anything you want, John cried.

And the worldly young lawyer-courtier-statesman
Metamorphosed into an ascetic who ate and slept sparingly,
Referring everything to the love of God.

Then the erstwhile governor became a sage
And stepped out onto the international stage.

World Youth Day in Madrid, 2011

Before an immense crowd of expectant young
Benedict XVI was holding colloquy
With selected youth who told him their personal woes.
His speech concerned, however, spiritual throes.

Suddenly wind, rain, hail and lightning
Lashed Benedict and the spectators to a pause.
The young people responded by shouting and jumping around;
They were determined that the event not go aground.

This frenzy kept up for an eternity.
The pope looked at his sodden address and reflected.
Over the loudspeaker a voice asked everyone to pray.
The storm stopped and they moved on to the next olé.

Young Artist Relations

Whitefish swimming in a watercolor sea,
A winter tree by a muskrat hollow,
A cottage in a billowing cornflower field,
February insects busy in the ground -
These are the drawings you have sent to me.
Over crumpets I contemplate your photographs,
And I fall in love all over again.

Made in the USA
Middletown, DE
24 March 2015